The MEMORY JOGGER™ 9000

A Pocket Guide to Implementing
the ISO 9000 Quality Systems Standard
and QS-9000 Requirements

Robert W. Peach
Robert Peach and Associates, Inc.
and
Diane S. Ritter
GOAL/QPC

First Edition
GOAL/QPC

The MEMORY JOGGER™ 9000

Robert W. Peach, Author
Principal, Robert Peach and Associates, Inc.

Diane Ritter, Author
GOAL/QPC

Francine Oddo, Editor
Michele Kierstead, Graphic Design
Lori Champney, Cover Design

GOAL/QPC
13 Branch Street, Methuen, MA 01844-1953
Toll free: 1-800-643-4316
Phone: 508-685-3900 Fax: 508-685-6151

Printed in the United States of America

First Edition
10 9 8 7 6 5 4 3 2 1

ISBN 1-879364-82-4

Acknowledgments

Our sincerest thanks to the people and organizations who have contributed their insights, suggestions, and encouragement or who gave us permission to use and adapt their tips, charts, tables, and other illustrative information.

Concept & Content Reviewers

Paul Amaral, *Texas Instruments, Inc.;* Captain Brian Basel, *U.S. Coast Guard Headquarters;* Michael Brassard, *GOAL/QPC;* Frank Caplan, *Quality Sciences Consultants, Inc.;* Tom Condardo, *ZBR Publications, Inc.;* Robin Crusse, *U.S. Coast Guard;* Ross Gilbert, *Kohler Company;* George Haire, *Mine Safety Applicances Co.;* Linda Johnson, *Allegro MicroSystems, Inc.;* Kevin Lange, *General Physics Corp.;* Johnny Morris, *Shep Enterprises;* Darwin Newell, *Dover Corp., Cook Division;* Paul O'Donnell, *U.S. Coast Guard;* Elizabeth Potts, *ABS QE;* Jan Pruett, *BellSouth Telecommunications, Inc.;* Gary Roberts, *Apple Computer, Inc.;* John Stratton, *Eastman Kodak;* Joseph Tsiakals, *Baxter Biotech.*

Contributors

Robert Belfit Jr., *Omni Tech International;* Jane Belmondo, *Quality Sciences Consultants, Inc.;* Frank Caplan, *Quality Science Consultants, Inc.;* David Erdman, *MacDermid, Inc.;* William Howarth, *D.B. Riley, Inc.;* Linda Johnson, *Allegro MicroSystems, Inc.;* Donald Marquardt, *Marquardt and Associates;* Sam Tolbert, *Scientific Atlanta;* William J. Vance, *Haworth, Inc.;* Steve Wirkus, *Advanced Cardiovascular Systems, Inc.*

Publishers

ASQC; Information Mapping; Irwin Professional Publishers; Marcel Dekker Publishers.

GOAL/QPC Project Team Members

Steve Boudreau; Michael Brassard; Paul Brassard; Deborah Crovo; Lisa Gilliland; Phil Kendall; Michele Kierstead; Stan Marsh; Richard Morrison; Francine Oddo; Dorie Overhoff; Robert Page; Diane Ritter, Project Manager.

Editor's Note

Authors Robert Peach and Diane Ritter have combined their talents to produce a readable, user-friendly guide for all of those involved in the process of adopting and using ISO 9000/QS-9000. Mr. Peach is an original member of the ISO committee that developed the ISO 9000 Quality Systems Standard, and editor of the *ISO 9000 Handbook*. Ms. Ritter is a co-author of *The Memory Jogger™*, *The Memory Jogger™ II*, and the *Coach's Guide to The Memory Jogger™ II*.

Authors' Note

From concept to publication, this book is the result of the collaborative effort of a "virtual" team. Phones, faxes, computers, postal mail, and e-mail all played a part in connecting the GOAL/QPC home office in Massachusetts to the writers in North Carolina and Georgia, and from the writers to the many friends and colleagues scattered across the nation.

All this was possible because of the quality and standardization of the many systems and processes in place. For that, we are grateful to the concepts and tools of Total Quality Management and ISO 9000 standards.

To our friends and colleagues who have read the manuscript or provided material, we thank you for your knowledge, thoughtfulness, honesty, insight, and suggestions.

And for the continued love, support, and extreme patience they have shown throughout this project, we owe a special note of thanks to:

Shirley Peach & Mary Ann Lee
Paul, Christian, Karin & Lauren Ritter

We are forever in your debt.

iv

Contents

Refer to the blue-edged pages for detailed contents.

How to Use The Memory Jogger™ 9000

The Memory Jogger™ 9000 is a convenient and quick reference guide on the job. It is intended to serve as a reminder of the things you have already learned through training, reading, or experience.

- To get an overview of what's in each chapter, check the "Contents" on page *v*.
- If you have a specific topic you're interested in, go to the chapter title pages for a detailed list of the contents. Each chapter title page has a blue edge.

Who Should Use This Book?

Much has been written to describe how to make use of the ISO 9000 Quality Systems Standard/QS-9000 Requirements. Almost all of these resources were written for *the few people* in an organization who are responsible for guiding the implementation effort, however, in the end, *every member of the company will be affected*.

Unlike these other resources, *The Memory Jogger™ 9000* was written for a broad audience, including managers, implementation teams, supervisors, staff, and all others who need to understand what *they* must do to actively contribute to the implementation and registration effort of ISO 9000/QS-9000.

Chapter 1

Introduction to ISO 9000

Customers and global competitiveness are changing the way organizations around the world are doing business. Quality is leading that change, providing quality products and services to keep your customers coming back. However, quality doesn't happen just because you talk about it.

To achieve quality you must work at it by understanding your processes—the work you do every day—and continually improving them.

Standardizing your work into an organized and documented system can provide the foundation for a comprehensive quality management program. ISO 9000 standards and QS-9000 Requirements are helping organizations do just that!

What does ISO mean?

ISO is recognized as the short name for the *International Organization for Standardization*, an international agency consisting of almost 100 member countries. Each country (no matter how small or how large) has one "equal" vote.

The United States' representative to ISO is the organization called the American National Standards Institute (ANSI). The ISO works to promote the development of standards, testing, and certification to encourage the trade of quality products and services: town to town, state to state, and country to country around the globe.

What is ISO 9000?

The core of the ISO 9000 Quality Systems Standard is a series of five international standards that provide guidance in the development and implementation of an effective quality management system. Not specific to any particular product, these standards are applicable to manufacturing and service industries alike.

A quality management system refers to the activities you carry out within your organization to satisfy the quality-related expectations of your customers. To ensure that you have a quality management system in place, customers or regulatory agencies may insist that your organization demonstrate that your quality management system conforms to one of the ISO 9000 quality system models. Then, the customer "second party," or an independent "third party" registrar comes into your organization to "audit," or verify, that you have such a system in place. When a registrar finds your organization fulfills the requirements of the ISO 9000 standards, your organization becomes "registered" and receives a certificate that is accepted by many of your customers. Companies not concerned with becoming registered may, nevertheless, want to comply with ISO 9000.

Complying with ISO 9000 standards does *not* indicate that every product or service meets the customers' requirements, only that the quality system in use is *capable* of meeting them. That is why you and your organization must continuously assess how satisfied your customers are and constantly improve the processes that produce the products or services.

The ISO 9000 Series

- **ISO 9000-1:** This standard provides guidelines and basic definitions that describe what the series is about and helps in the selection and use of the appropriate ISO standard (ISO 9001, 9002, or 9003) for any organization.

- **ISO 9001:** This standard is a model for use by organizations (both manufacturing and service) to certify their quality system from initial design and development of a desired product or service through production, installation, and servicing.

- **ISO 9002:** This standard is identical to ISO 9001 except it omits the requirement of documenting the design/development process.

- **ISO 9003:** This standard is for use by organizations that need only to show, through inspection and testing, that they are delivering the desired product or service.

- **ISO 9004-1:** This standard is a basic set of guidelines that organizations can use to help them develop and implement their quality management system.

Whereas ISO 9001, ISO 9002, and ISO 9003 are requirements, ISO 9004-1 is a guideline. The ISO requirements describe *what* must be done to make up a quality management system, not *how* to set it up.

Note: *ISO 9001 is the most comprehensive and includes the contents of ISO 9002 and ISO 9003. This book will present the contents of ISO 9001 only.*

ISO 9001 consists of 20 sections called *clauses* (see the next page). These requirements spell out what your organization and possibly you must do to conform to the standard. All the requirements must be documented and controlled.

The QS-9000 Requirements

QS-9000 is a supplement to ISO 9001, developed by the automotive Big Three—Chrysler, Ford, and General Motors—and available through the Automotive Industry Action Group (AIAG). These manufacturers are requiring their first-tier suppliers to adopt the QS-9000 Requirements, which incorporate the entire ISO 9001 standard. In addition, five reference manuals have been published that complete the documents describing the QS-9000 Quality System Requirements (see page 157).

Note: *In Chapters 1 and 2, general references to ISO 9000 or ISO 9001 include QS-9000. The wording for ISO 9001 and QS-9000 has been paraphrased in Chapter 3. An effort has been made **not to change the meaning** of the requirements of the standard. For actual phrasing, please refer to the texts of ISO 9001 and QS-9000, as well as ISO 9000-2 "Generic Guidelines for the Application of ISO 9000."*

Clauses in the ISO 9001 Quality Systems Standard

4.1 Management responsibility

4.2 Quality system

4.3 Contract review

4.4 Design control

4.5 Document and data control

4.6 Purchasing

4.7 Control of customer-supplied product

4.8 Product identification and traceability

4.9 Process control

4.10 Inspection and testing

4.11 Control of inspection, measuring, and test equipment

4.12 Inspection and test status

4.13 Control of nonconforming product

4.14 Corrective and preventive action

4.15 Handling, storage, packaging, preservation, and delivery

4.16 Control of quality records

4.17 Internal quality audits

4.18 Training

4.19 Servicing

4.20 Statistical techniques

Why are we adopting ISO 9000?

Organizations adopt ISO 9000 standards for different reasons. Your organization's decision to do so may include:

- To comply with customers who require ISO 9000
- To sell in the European Union (EU) markets
- To compete in domestic and worldwide markets
- To improve your quality system
- To minimize repetitive auditing by similar and different customers
- To improve subcontractors' performance

Global benefits include:

- A widening acceptance of the standards
- A worldwide availability of the standards in many languages, which enhances communication between multinational customers and suppliers

Both you and your organization benefit since use of ISO 9000 serves as a basis to:

- Achieve better understanding and consistency of all quality practice throughout the organization
- Ensure continued use of the required quality system year after year
- Improve documentation
- Improve quality awareness
- Strengthen supplier/customer confidence and relationships
- Yield cost savings and improve profitability
- Form a foundation and discipline for improvement activities within TQM

Of course, these benefits are achieved only with good planning, hard work, and continuous improvement.

Key Terms

Supplier/Organization/Subcontractor

ISO 9001, 9002, and 9003 use the term *supplier* in reference to your organization. This is because the requirement standards are external, written from the view of the customer or "third-party" registrar. Sometimes your organization is referred to as the "first-party."

ISO 9004-1, the guideline standard, is an internal standard, consequently it uses the term *organization* to refer to you.

Subcontractor refers to the organization from which you purchase materials, parts, assemblies, and services.

Certification Versus Registration

Certification has multiple meanings and usages:

- Individuals may be *certified* to certain tasks: welder, forklift/truck operator, nurse, CPA, paramedic, etc.

- Individually manufactured products or services may be *certified*, such as raw materials with quality attested to by a test certificate.

- The existence and proper operation of an ISO 9000 quality system may be *certified* with a certificate issued by an accredited registrar.

The process of confirming usage of ISO 9000 has been widely referred to, particularly in Europe, as *certification.* The multiple usages of the term "certification" can be confusing, particularly because use of ISO 9000 does not certify that every product meets specification requirements, only that the quality system in use is capable of meeting requirements. To avoid confusion, the term *registration* is preferable in referring to the process of meeting the ISO 9000 requirements. That usage is followed throughout this text.

Preparing for ISO 9000 Registration

No single sequence exists that all organizations must follow to achieve registration to ISO 9000, since the process depends upon the state of each organization's quality practice.

Three basic requirements of the ISO 9000 standards are:

1. Document your processes that affect quality.

2. Retain records and data that describe the quality of the product or service.

3. Ensure that your processes produce consistent quality.

A familiar sequence toward registration is:

> *Say* what you do.
> *Do* what you say.
> *Prove* it.
> *Improve* it!

However, your organization should judge whether the improvement stage should occur before documentation. If so, that sequence is characterized as follows:

- Digest the contents of ISO 9000.
- Discover the best way to operate.
- Document your quality practice.
- Deploy your procedures.
- Demonstrate your actions to the registrar.

Contributed by Jane Belmondo, Quality Sciences Consultants, Inc.

Whichever process your organization chooses, always be alert to opportunities for improvements in practice: before, during, and after ISO 9000 registration!

Steps to Registration

The following is a generic process that organizations tend to follow to achieve ISO 9000 quality system registration.

Phase I Organizing for Registration
- Obtain management commitment.
- Establish a steering team. Its role is to:
  - assign responsibilities
  - determine ISO standard to be used
  - determine if other requirements or standards are to be used (QS-9000, ISO 9004-1, customer-specific standards)
  - identify sites involved
  - establish a budget
  - set a timetable
  - determine if an external consultant will be used; if so, hire one
- Train key team (externally or in-house seminar).
- Begin internal quality auditing.
- Select a registrar; contact registrar representative; obtain registrar information packet.

Phase II Preparing for Registration
- Document existing processes with quality procedures and work/job instructions.
- Identify areas needing improvement.
- Adopt improved quality procedures and work/job instructions.
- Prepare the quality manual.
- Apply to your registrar for an assessment; pay any necessary application fee.
- Submit the quality manual to the registrar for review.
- Arrange to have a pre-assessment conducted by your registrar (optional); set assessment date.

- Respond to the pre-assessment recommendations.
- Conduct a "dress rehearsal" audit.
- Submit your revised manual to the registrar.
- Modify and finalize quality practices; train personnel.

Phase III Experiencing the Registration Audit

- Arrange for your registrar to conduct the assessment and identify findings (discrepancies).
- Respond to the findings.
- Submit to the registrar for review the corrective actions you will take.
- The registration certificate is awarded.

Phase IV Continuing Registration Through Surveillance Audits

- Maintain quality practice to ensure continued compliance.
- Notify your registrar of major changes in practice.
- Arrange for registrar to conduct semi-annual surveillance audits.
- Continue to improve.

Lessons Learned

Most organizations will find that adopting ISO 9001 and QS-9000 helps in:

- Gaining a complete understanding of all operations from a customer point of view.
- Identifying opportunities for process improvement.

An effective approach to getting ready for ISO 9000 and QS-9000 registration is to follow the Plan-Do-Check-Act Cycle (see Chapter 2, page 26).

Chapter 2

Getting Ready for ISO 9000

What does it mean for me?

ISO 9000 is about knowing and understanding your customers (both internal and external) and their requirements, and then ensuring that your work meets those requirements.

Your work is defined by one or more processes: a series of repeatable steps that result in an outcome—some defined product or service.

As your organization gets involved in implementing ISO 9000 standards, you may be asked to:

- Participate, or assist, in identifying the work that you do that affects the quality of the products or services your organization provides your customer(s)

- Improve your work processes

- Write procedures that describe your work

- Keep records and data

- Participate in internal audits

- Participate in external registration and surveillance audits if your organization goes for ISO 9000 registration

To understand the sequencing and activities that will involve you, follow the ISO 9000 flowchart on the next page.

ISO 9000 Process Flowchart

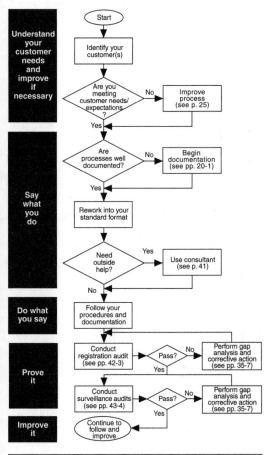

Understand your customer needs and improve if necessary

Start

Identify your customer(s)

Are you meeting customer needs/expectations? — No → Improve process (see p. 25)

Yes ↓

Say what you do

Are processes well documented? — No → Begin documentation (see pp. 20-1)

Yes ↓

Rework into your standard format

Need outside help? — Yes → Use consultant (see p. 41)

No ↓

Do what you say

Follow your procedures and documentation

Prove it

Conduct registration audit (see pp. 42-3) → Pass? — No → Perform gap analysis and corrective action (see pp. 35-7)

Yes ↓

Conduct surveillance audits (see pp. 43-4) → Pass? — No → Perform gap analysis and corrective action (see pp. 35-7)

Yes ↓

Improve it

Continue to follow and improve

ISO 9001 Helps Satisfy
Internal and External Customers

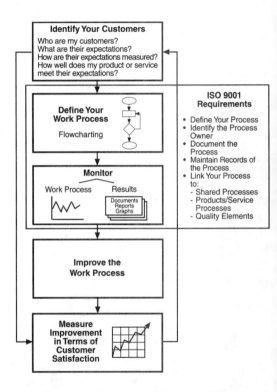

Identify Your Customers

Who are my customers?
What are their expectations?
How are their expectations measured?
How well does my product or service
meet their expectations?

**Define Your
Work Process**

Flowcharting

Monitor

Work Process   Results

Documents
Reports
Graphs

**Improve the
Work Process**

**Measure
Improvement
in Terms of
Customer
Satisfaction**

**ISO 9001
Requirements**

- Define Your Process
- Identify the Process Owner
- Document the Process
- Maintain Records of the Process
- Link Your Process to:
  - Shared Processes
  - Products/Service Processes
  - Quality Elements

*Information provided courtesy of William Howarth,
D.B. Riley, Inc., Worcester, MA*

©1996 GOAL/QPC

Documentation

A key to getting ready for ISO 9000 and QS-9000 registration is to follow the sequence of the Plan-Do-Check-Act (PDCA) Cycle. Each step toward registration can follow the PDCA Cycle: documentation, the process-improvement model (see page 26), registration audit, and surveillance audits.

Since it is a continual cycle, it is sometimes appropriate to start at "Check" for a Check-Act-Plan-Do Cycle. The quality system documentation process would then follow the following sequence:

CHECK	Understand the contents of the standard.
ACT	Determine the need for system improvement before preparing documentation for ISO 9000 registration.
PLAN	Establish a schedule for training and development of documentation.
DO	Document the quality system sufficiently to be able to demonstrate its operation to a third-party registrar.

Documentation required for ISO 9000 and QS-9000 can be identified in four levels.

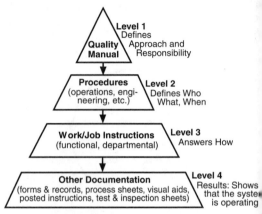

Adapted from the QS-9000 Quality Systems Requirements, p. 3

Level 1: **Quality Manual**–Statement of the organization's quality policy, written by managers from top-level management and the quality department.

Level 2: **Procedures**–Defines activities at the departmental level and written by department supervisors.

Level 3: **Work/Job Instructions**–Describes how jobs are accomplished and are usually written by the operators and trainers.

Level 4: **Other Documentation**–A compilation of forms (hard copy and/or electronic) used in the quality system. This is usually done by quality and/or middle managers.

Level 1: Preparing the Quality Manual

The quality manual is the top level of your organization's documentation system. It states your organization's policy on, and commitment to, quality. Ideally built around the structure of ISO 9000, the quality manual provides the content and index for all of the documentation, including procedures and job instructions. The body of the quality manual usually consists of a page or two for each of the applicable clauses of the ISO 9000 standard. The quality manual is written by your top-level managers and quality department managers.

Typical Outline of a Quality Manual

- Quality Policy
- Organizational Chart
- Quality Organization
- Statement of Authority and Responsibility
- Distribution List of Controlled Copies
- Quality System, Clauses 4.1–4.20
- Procedures Index
- Forms Index (Included or referenced)

See ISO 10013: 1994, "Guidelines for Developing Quality Manuals."

▲ Level 2:
Preparing Quality Procedures

Procedures are the second level of the quality documentation pyramid. Written by the department supervisors, they describe activities typically at the departmental level, and their relationship to the supplier operations as a whole. You will, more than likely participate in the preparation of your procedures and/or work/job instructions. Procedures should ideally be organized into the ISO 9001 outline structure, indicating the ISO 9001 clause (4.1–4.20) under which they fall, though this is not an ISO 9001 requirement. A sequence for developing quality procedures appears on the next page.

Typical Outline of a Quality Procedure

- **Purpose/Objective:** aim of the procedure

- **Scope:** what the procedure does and does not cover

- **Responsibilities:** who (by job function) has responsibilities for specific tasks or actions

- **References:** to all documents covered under the procedure

- **Definitions:** of key terms or acronyms

- **Procedures:** description of the actions or tasks to be carried out, by whom, and in what sequence

- **Documentation:** what documentation is needed

In certain cases, Level 2 procedures and Level 3 work/job instructions can be combined.

Quality Procedure Writing Process Flowchart

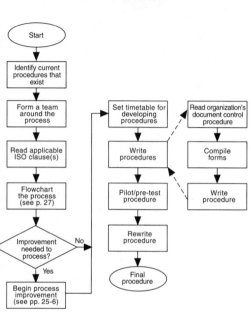

Start

Identify current procedures that exist

Form a team around the process

Read applicable ISO clause(s)

Flowchart the process (see p. 27)

Improvement needed to process? — No

Yes

Begin process improvement (see pp. 25-6)

Set timetable for developing procedures

Write procedures

Pilot/pre-test procedure

Rewrite procedure

Final procedure

Read organization's document control procedure

Compile forms

Write procedure

Suggestions for Writing Documentation

Procedures, Work/Job Instructions, and Other Documentation

- Keep it short and simple. Don't "over-document."

- Flowchart a process, if appropriate (see pp. 27-9). Make extensive use of charts and tables.

- Use a standardized format.

- Keep the audience in mind:

  - Make the meaning very clear; have someone else read it and explain back what you said.

  - Make the text grammatically correct.

  - Search out errors in spelling and punctuation.

  - Avoid jargon.

  - Separate ideas into individual sentences or paragraphs.

  - Write to the task, not an individual. Documents are written to help workers perform their tasks more efficiently and consistently.

  - Ask the user to help write the documentation, where possible.

- For every task, identify:

  - Who is responsible for making sure that it is done

  - Standards to be met/completion criteria

  - What resources are needed

  - What records are kept

  - What to do if it doesn't work

- Pre-test procedures. Have those who will use them try them and provide feedback.

Sample Procedure

Document Control Procedure

Purpose
This document describes the procedure to be followed for the approval, issue, and maintenance of all controlled documentation.

Scope
This procedure shall apply to all controlled documentation relating to all company products and services.

References
    Document Change Procedure DOC-PROC-001
    Document Register DOC-REG-001

Procedure
All controlled documentation shall be subject to approval by the following before issue and release:
    a) Originator
    b) Originator's manager
    c) Quality manager

Released documentation can only be changed in accordance with the Change Control System DOC-PROC-001.

A record of all controlled documentation shall be maintained by the quality manager indicating the following:
    a) Reference number
    b) Issue number
    c) Disposition of copies.

Details of controlled document holders shall be held on the Document Register.

Officially distributed copies of the documents shall be identified by a red "Official Distribution" stamp giving date of distribution. Action affecting product quality shall only be taken on the basis of information contained in officially distributed copies of controlled documents.

Master copies of all controlled documentation shall be held by the quality manager.

All copies of documentation that become obsolete by reissue shall be promptly removed from distribution. One copy shall be archived by the quality manager; all other copies shall be destroyed.

From The ISO 9000 Handbook,
Irwin Professional Publishing, Chapter 7,
Quality System Documentation, 1994, p. 239

Level 3: Preparing Work/Job Instructions

Work or job instructions are the third level of documentation. They describe how work is accomplished and are usually written by the operators and trainers. You will probably find that you already have instructions for many of your key operations.

Follow the directions for writing documentation listed on page 20. Use the following list of points when you are documenting your work.

Work/Job Instructions

- Start from existing written work/job instructions.
- Consider using the team approach in preparing instructions.
- Verify that existing instructions describe the present activity. If not, correct them.
- Determine whether present practice is satisfactory or a quality improvement process should be followed.
- Adopt improved practice, if necessary.
- Flowchart complex operations.
- Begin upgrading and evaluating the job instructions.
- Verify that work/job instructions are being followed after work/job is completed.
- Use work/job instructions as a basis for training.

Sample Work/Job Instruction

Tank Car Wash Rack and Inspection

Document no.: TKWR02	**Description:** Tank car wash and inspection
Revision no.: 0	**Sheet:** 1 of 3
Prepared by: Paul Brown	**Approved by:** T. Jones
Issued by: Cleaning Section	**Issue Date:** May 31, 1991

1.0 Introduction

Prior to loading, most tank cars are washed and internally and externally inspected. Cars that are recycled for specified products (list) are not washed. These recycled tanks are controlled (how) by the shipping services supervisor.

2.0 Preparation

1. Switching crew selects tank car.
2. Secure tank car by chock and hand brakes.
3. Connect ground cables to each car.
4. Attach safety appliances to each car.
5. Depressurize all pressurized tanks.
6. Manway bottom outlet valves.
7. Open: Secondary valves.
   Vent valves
   Induction valves
8. Remove cap from bottom outlet valve nozzle.

From ISO 9000: Preparing for Registration, James L. Lamprecht, Marcel Dekker, NY, 1992, p. 95

A "controlled document" will have:
- **ⓐ Title**
- **ⓑ Document number** (a unique identifier)
- **ⓒ Revision indicator** (e.g., Rev. A, -001, B, [blank])
- **ⓓ Page number** (e.g., Page 1 of 3, Page 1.2, 1-2.3)
- **ⓔ Date issued/revised** (e.g., April 6, 1996, 4/6/96)
- **ⓕ Approval** (the approving authority by signature and perhaps also position title)
- **ⓖ Prepared by/Issued by** (name, position, and/or department)

Level 4:
Preparing Other Documentation

Level four consists of all forms, or controlled documents and quality records (hard copy and/or electronic) necessary for the quality system to operate. Compilation of a current file of these forms involves middle managers and quality managers. For each of the ISO 9001 clauses, this section of the manual lists the required documentation.

Examples of Other Quality Forms

- Quality Policy
- Quality Objectives and Commitment
- Organization Chart
- Receiving Record
- Warranty and Repair Tag
- Repair/Warranty Log
- Repair Order Form
- Discrepancy Report
- Bill of Materials
- Phoned-In Sales Order
- Design Requirements
- Major Customer Forecast
- Purchase Order
- Subcontractor Review
- Product Release Stamp
- Storage Assessment
- Internal Quality Audit
- New Employee Orientation
- Certificate of Training

Improving Work Processes

At some point you may need to improve your work and work processes. This may occur if you:

- Are not meeting your customer needs and requirements
- Have not satisfied the requirements of the registration or surveillance audits
- Just want to be better

To help you do this, use:

- **Problem-Solving/Process-Improvement Model**
  A systematic approach to focus on a problem, identify root cause(s), and develop and implement solutions and action plans. (See next page.)

- **Flowcharting a Process**
  A graphic tool for documenting and understanding the flow or sequence of events in your work process. (See pages 27–9.)

- **Process Control System**
  The use of data as feedback on how a process is performing. (See pages 30–2.)

- **Collecting, Organizing, and Reporting Data and Information**
  In problem solving/process improvement, controlled documentation, and record keeping, you will need to understand some basic points on collecting data and how best to present the data graphically. (See pages 33–5.)

- **Gap Analysis**
  Identifying missing process elements or undocumented procedures. (See pages 35–7.)

Note: *Also see ISO 9004-4 (10004) "Guidelines for Quality Improvement."*

Problem-Solving/
Process-Improvement Model

There are many standard models for making improvements. They all attempt to provide a repeatable set of steps that a team or individual can learn and follow. The improvement storyboard is only one of many models that include typical steps using typical tools. Follow this model or any other model that creates a common language for continuous improvement within your organization.

Plan

1. Select the problem/process that will be addressed first (or next) and describe the improvement opportunity.

2. Describe the current process surrounding the improvement opportunity.

3. Describe all of the possible causes of the problem and agree on the root cause(s).

4. Develop an effective and workable solution and action plan, including targets for improvement.

Do

5. Implement the solution or process change.

Check

6. Review and evaluate the result of the change.

Act

7. Reflect and act on learnings.

From The Memory Jogger™ II,
GOAL/QPC, 1994, p. 115

Flowcharting a Process

The flowchart allows you or a team to identify the actual flow or sequence of events in a process that any product or service follows. A flowchart helps uncover unexpected complexity in the process, allowing you to come to understand the actual process steps, and then work to identify improvement opportunities or locations where additional data can be collected and investigated.

How do I do it?

See *The Memory Jogger™ II* and the *Coach's Guide to The Memory Jogger™ II* for more detail on construction and interpretation.

1. **Determine the frame or boundaries of the process.**
   - Clearly define the start and end of the process.
   - Determine the level of detail needed to clearly understand the process and identify problem areas.

2. **Determine the steps in the process.**
   - Brainstorm a list of all major activities, inputs, outputs, and decisions from the beginning to the end of the process.

3. **Sequence the steps.**
   - Arrange the steps in the order they are carried out.
   - Unless flowcharting a new process, sequence what *is*, not what *should* be.

4. **Draw the flowchart using the appropriate symbols (see chart on next page).**
   - Keep the flowchart simple.
   - Be consistent in the level of detail shown.
   - Label each process step using words that everyone understands.

5. **Test the flowchart for completeness.**
   - Are the symbols used correctly?
   - Are the process steps identified clearly?
   - Make sure every feedback loop is closed.

Flowchart Symbols

Symbol	Represents	Detail/Example
⬭	Start/End Input/Output	Request for proposal, request for new hire, raw material
▢	Task, action, execution point	Hold a meeting, make a phone call, open a box
◇ ?	Decision point	Yes/no Accept/reject Pass/fail Criteria met/not met
▱	Document	A report or form is filled out, job request, meeting minutes
▢	Shadow signifies additional flowchart for this task	A major task has subtasks not needed for this study or subtasks not included due to limited space
◗	Delay	Waiting for service, report sitting on a desk
→Ⓐ Ⓐ→	Continuation	Go to another page, go to another part of the chart
→	Arrow	Shows direction or flow of the process steps

From the Coach's Guide to The Memory Jogger™ II,
GOAL/QPC, 1995, p. 70

- Check that every continuation point has a corresponding point elsewhere.
- Use only one arrow out of an activity box. If there is more than one arrow, you may need a decision diamond.
- Validate the flowchart with people who carry out the process actions.

6. **Finalize the flowchart.**
   - Is the process being run the way it should be?
   - Are people following the process as charted?
   - Are there obvious complexities or redundancies that can be reduced or eliminated?
   - How different is the current process from ideal? Draw an ideal flowchart and compare the two to identify discrepancies and opportunities for improvements.

Receiving Materials Flowchart

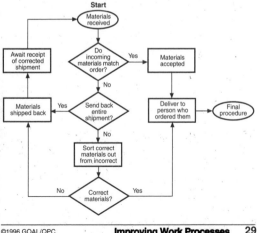

Process Control System

A process control system is the continual cycle of using data as feedback on the performance of a process to identify the sources of variation and then working to reduce or eliminate this variation. Doing so results in improved outputs that better meet your customers' defined quality of product and service.

All work that we do is a process. There are definable inputs, steps, and decisions that produce outputs of products and services for our customers. Unfortunately, no two outputs are exactly alike. They vary from each other due to variations of the inputs: people, equipment, materials, methods, and environment.

Sources of variation can be grouped into two major classes:

- *Common cause* is a source of variation that is always present; part of the random variation inherent in the process itself. Its origin can usually be traced to an element of the process that only management can correct; it is beyond the control of the operator.

- *Special cause* is a source that is intermittent, localized, seasonal, unpredictable, unstable. Its origin can usually be traced to an element of the system that can be corrected locally, that is, an employee or operator may be able to correct a special cause.

Control charts help separate out these two sources of variation and identify who has responsibility for correcting them: management (common cause) or local operators, subcontractors, machines, equipment, etc. (special cause).

Control Chart

A control chart is a graphical tool that allows you to "visibly track" variation in a process over time. It is important to monitor changes in process variation in order to control the process. A process must be in statistical control before you can improve it.

A process is said to be in a state of statistical control, or "in control," when measurements from the process vary randomly within statistically calculated limits. That is, there are no points outside the limits and no points forming trend lines, shifts, cycles, or other patterns. Over time, the variation present is consistent and predictable.

A process that consistently and predictably produces product or service within three standard deviations (the statistically calculated "control limits") of the mean is considered to be in a state of statistical control. This means that all special causes of variation within the process have been removed.

Note that a process "in control" may not be producing good product or service, however, only that it is consistent and predictable. It could be consistent and predictably bad!

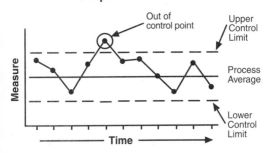

Simple Control Chart

Process Capability

Process capability is used to determine whether a process, given its natural variation, is capable of meeting established customer requirements or specifications. It helps you answer the questions, "Is the process capable of meeting the requirement?" "Has there been a change in the process?" "What percentage of my product or service is not meeting the customer requirement?"

Capability indices have been developed to compare the distribution of your process in relation to the customer specification limits. Before capability can be determined, a stable process must be obtained. A stable process can be represented by a measure of its variation—six standard deviations. Comparing six standard deviations of the process variation to the customer specification provides a measure of capability. Some measures of capability include C_p (simple) and its inverse C_r, C_{pl}, and C_{pu} for single-sided specification limits, and C_{pk} (uses $3\hat{\sigma}$) for two-sided specification limits.

Calculation, construction, and interpretation of control charts and process capability are beyond the scope of this book. For more detailed information, see *The Memory Jogger™ II*, or the *Fundamental Statistical Process Control Reference Manual* by the automotive Big Three, (Chrysler, Ford, and General Motors), or other statistical books. The five Customer Reference Manuals referred to in QS-9000 are listed on page 157.

Collecting, Organizing, and Reporting Data and Information

As you become involved in implementing your quality system, one of your responsibilities may include collecting, organizing, and reporting data and information about your work/process. Data and information are collected to document a current situation, as well as to understand how the process is performing and what action needs to be taken to control, fix, or improve it.

Collecting data

- Clarify the purpose of the problem and focus only on what you need or what's required.

- Make sure the data represent the process. Know what type of data or information you have; the data will often dictate the tool you will use or the way to display it.

- Stratify data if necessary, e.g., separate it by days, machines, types, etc.

- Keep data collection and information forms simple.

- Use historical data first, if available. This will set a baseline of past performance.

Organizing/reporting data and information

The tool you should use to organize and report data depends on the *type* of data you have or plan to collect; data can be words or numbers, and either counted or measured. Use the Tool and Data Chart on the next page to help you decide on the most appropriate tool.

Statistical data

Predictable patterns or distributions of data can be described with statistics. These include:

- Measures of location (mean, median, mode)
- Measures of variation (range, standard deviation)

Tool and Data Chart

Number Data (Count or attribute)	Tool to Use
• Show frequency of events	• Check Sheet • Pareto
• Show process performance over time	• Run Chart • Control Chart
• Show capability of process to meet customer requirements	• Process Capability

Number Data (Measure or variable)	Tool to Use
• Show relationship among multiple data sets over time	• Radar Chart • Run Chart
• Show centering and variation of a process	• Histogram
• Show correlations between two or more data sets	• Scatter
• Show process performance over time	• Run Chart • Control Chart
• Show capability of process to meet customer requirements	• Process Capability

Continued on next page

Refer to *The Memory Jogger™ II, Coach's Guide to The Memory Jogger™ II,* or other statistical books for guidance on selection, construction, and interpretation of the quality control and management and planning tools.

Word Data	Tool to Use
• Show process flow	• AND • Gantt • Flowchart
• Generate ideas	• Brainstorming
• Narrow Ideas	• NGT/Multivoting
• Sort ideas	• Affinity • Cause & Effect • Force Field
• Show relationships	• Cause & Effect • Interrelationship
• Show greater level of detail	• Cause & Effect • Tree Diagram
• Show correlations	• Cause & Effect • Force Field • Interrelationship • Prioritization • Radar Chart
• Develop consensus	• Matrix Diagram • Prioritization
• Plan contingencies	• PDPC

Gap Analysis

ISO 9000 requires that every applicable requirement of the standard be met and all procedures be adequately documented. This calls for a system-wide structure that links all activities effectively, ensuring a smooth flow of information throughout the organization.

The process of identifying missing process elements or undocumented procedures is called *gap analysis*. This is part of a full-scale audit of current practice against relevant sections of the ISO 9001 standard and company documentation. Gap analysis is typically conducted in the preparation period before the visit by the registrar who will determine your conformity to the standard. It is appropriate *at any time* to evaluate the conformity of your quality system to ISO 9001. Findings of the gap analysis provide you with a basis for acting to ensure that all quality system elements are being addressed.

Typical Findings of a Gap Analysis

- There are inadequate work instructions and quality control information for people doing production, inspection, and test.

- Procedures and work instructions are not followed.

- Changes on controlled drawings and documents are unauthorized.

- There are no procedures for dealing with obsolete drawings and documents.

- The corrective action taken with subcontractors who provide defective material and parts is inadequate.

- There is no management support for follow through on corrective action issues.

- Material in the storeroom is out of date, damaged, corroded, unidentified, unprotected, or nonconforming.

- There are no work instructions for repair, rework, and reinspection.

- Statistical methods are used incorrectly.

Information provided courtesy of David Erdman, Macdermid, Inc., Waterbury, CT. He was with DuPont Electronics when he compiled this information.

Gap Analysis and Corrective Action Process

	Stage	What the Team Does
Gap Analysis	1	• Identifies the requirements of the selected conformance model (ISO 9001, 9002, or 9003) • Identifies any corporate, regulatory, or statutory requirements
	2	Resolves any differences between the requirements of the conformance model and any applicable • regulatory requirements • statutory requirements • corporate requirements
	3	Identifies the existing process in the quality system **Note:** There may not be an existing process.
	4	• Identifies documents that support the existing process • Compares documents to the existing process • Resolves conflicts between process and documents
	5	Compares the existing quality system to the external requirements to identify any gaps
Corrective Action	6	Develops any necessary changes to existing process to close the gaps and obtains approval from management
	7	Develops new documents or changes existing documents as necessary and obtains approval from management
	8	Assists management in training of personnel and implementation of changes
	9	• Verifies effectiveness of any changes over time • Repeats Stages 5 through 8 as necessary to correct ineffective changes

From Demystifying ISO 9000, Information Mapping's Guide to the ISO 9000 Standards, *pp.4-6, 4-7*

Getting Ready for Registration

While preparing for and going through registration, you may come into contact with people both inside and outside you organization. To best use everyone's expertise, manage your time effectively with them, and have good working relationships, it is important to understand everyone's part in the implementation and registration process.

The roles and responsibilities of everyone in your organization include:

- Commiting to, and supporting, the ISO 9000 implementation effort
- Having a cooperative, positive attitude
- Communicating the status of the effort

Other roles and responsibilities

Staff/associates/line personnel
- Provide input to and verify that documented procedures are adequate and accurate.
- Know where the documents are located.
- Understand and use your work/job instructions.
- Know your organization's quality policy.
- Be aware of the appropriate ISO 9000 requirements.
- Direct any questions to the implementation team, the ISO 9000 coordinator, or your manager or supervisor.

Local Champions
- Act as task leader and technical resource.
- Identify and obtain required documentation.
- Evaluate the documentation for conformance to the standard.

Continued on next page

- Implement any necessary changes.
- Present status at progress review meetings.
- Participate in internal audits.
- Act as a key contact for ongoing support.

ISO 9000 Coordinator/Implementation Team
- Coordinate the registration process.
- Oversee training of all staff.
- Develop the format of the quality manual.
- Monitor and provide counsel for interpretation.
- Coordinate internal audits.
- Chair regular ISO 9000 progress review meetings.
- Report progress.

Managers
- Ensure effectiveness of quality systems within your areas.

Senior Management
- Commitment is key to success.
- Help develop and promote the organization's quality policy.
- Review progress.
- Provide resources.
- Ensure attainment of ISO 9000 registration.

Adapted from Linda Johnson,
Allegro MicroSystems, Inc., Worcester, MA

Role of the Registrar

Registrars are independent companies authorized to evaluate the capability of your organization to meet the ISO 9000 and QS-9000 Requirements. Auditors, who are qualified persons trained in the ISO 9000 standards, come into your organization and validate that you satisfy (or "comply with") the requirements. They audit your organization for the initial registrations, and return periodically to confirm that you continue to comply with the requirements. These are called surveillance audits.

Selecting a Registrar

- Make sure the registrar is accredited. If you will be operating in an international market, make sure the chosen registrar meets internationally accepted requirements.
- Consider whether you need a registrar with expertise in a particular industry.
- Will the registrar be responsive to your needs?
- What types of services does the registrar offer? Training courses? Tailored preliminary audits?
- What is the registrar's track record and reputation?
- How does the registrar train and maintain consistency of its assessors?
- What costs are involved (initial and long term)?
- How does the registrar respond to noncompliances?

Working with a Registrar/Auditor(s)

- *Do* get to know them since they will be coming back periodically.
- *Do* remember that, to the registrar, *you* are the customer.
- *Do* respond efficiently and effectively to auditors' inquiries.
- *Do* understand your processes, procedures, records, and data.
- *Do* go into a meeting with the auditor well prepared.

Continued on next page

- **Don't** look to the registrar for how to fix a finding. Registrars are not to serve as consultants.

- **Don't** try to lead the auditor or control the audit.

- **Don't** be afraid to answer a question with *"I don't know."* However, do say that you will find out the answer and get back to them as quickly as possible.

Role of the Consultant

Many organizations achieve ISO 9000 registration without using outside consultants, however, using one may be a good investment. With knowledge, field experience, and understanding of the ISO 9000 standards and QS-9000 Requirements as well as your business and industry, they can be valuable resources. Consultants often help plan the implementation effort, conduct training, and assist you and your organization to prepare for an audit. Also, they do not get distracted from the ISO 9000 process because of day-to-day business.

Working with a Consultant

- Ask for help in understanding how to implement ISO 9000; don't ask the consultant to do your job.

- Ask questions to help clarify any misunderstandings you may have on any of the ISO 9000 standards and QS-9000 Requirements that apply to you.

- Ask for pointers on writing your job description or documenting your process(es).

- Ask for advice on how to conduct yourself during an audit.

The Registration Audit

Audits are a way of obtaining objective feedback on how effective your quality system is: what's working well, what can be improved, and what isn't fulfilling your planned levels of performance.

- *Internal audits* are self-audits that help your organization "be ready" for the external audit conducted by your chosen registrar. They determine where your organization needs more training, more practice, or where a procedure may need to be revised and improved.
- *External audits* are when your chosen registrar officially comes in to verify that you conform to your selected ISO 9000 standard.

Prior to the Audit

- Submit your quality manual in advance.
- Respond to any modifications noted by the registrar.
- Consider arranging for a pre-assessment visit by the auditor. This isn't a consulting visit, but an observation as to whether you are ready for the registration audit, with suggestions on how to strengthen your system.
- Conduct a dress rehearsal. Review all elements of the registration audit to ensure that ISO 9000 requirements are being met.
- Train all members of the organization on how to respond to questions from auditors.

During the Audit

- Auditors will meet first with upper management to provide an overview of the registration event.
- Auditors will then circulate throughout the organization to determine whether your quality system is in accordance with your selected ISO 9000 standard.
- Auditors will observe the operations and ask questions concerning the work/job: *"How are you doing it? Are you following the procedures you have documented?"*

- Respond to questions honestly. Don't mislead or give uninformed replies.
- Make sure that you are following your procedures.

After the Audit
- Deal with auditor findings in a professional manner.
- Address any noncompliances in a positive way, correcting them and reporting back to the auditor in a timely way.
- Celebrate when you receive your certificate.
- Continue to review and improve your quality system.

Surveillance Audits

ISO 9000 registration systems require periodic surveillance to ensure that they continue in good running order. The focus of surveillance audits by registrars is to ensure continued compliance with the ISO 9000 standard. Auditors look for evidence that the quality system is being maintained in its entirety and improved and corrected as needed. Organizations that are continually maintaining and improving their quality system are sure to be in good shape to pass surveillance audits.

Surveillance audits include:

- Review of complaints
- Findings from internal audits
- Verification of corrective action
- Assessment of any changes that have taken place in the quality system

Expect most clauses of the quality system, document control, and record keeping to be reviewed on each visit. Not all registrars will review every clause of the ISO 9000 standard on every visit. If not, they will cover all the clauses over a predetermined period, such as three years. In most cases, registrars perform surveillance visits twice a year.

If a major nonconformity is uncovered during a surveillance visit, the auditor will work with you on the required corrective action, to avoid the necessity of withdrawing your registration certificate until corrective action has taken place.

Surveillance audits supplement the two activities that you, the supplier, conduct to ensure continued conformance to ISO 9000 requirements, the Internal Quality Audit (clause 4.17), and Management Review (sub-clause 4.1.3).

Across all levels and all functions, here's a checklist of key areas, questions, and tasks that your organization should consider when getting ready for the registration audit.

ISO 9000 Preparation Checklist

Area of Preparation	✔	Questions/ Tasks
Quality Manual	❑ ❑	Is it complete? Does it contain all elements that you want to be registered? Other standards in addition to the ISO 9000 standards?
Application for Registration	❑ ❑ ❑	Have you selected your registrar? Have you completed the application for registration and assessment? Does this company provide the long-term relationship you are seeking?
Internal Audits	❑ ❑	Have you reviewed all recent (last two years) internal audits to ensure that all items are closed? Were there any systems issues that should be re-reviewed at this time?
Audit Agenda	❑	Has this been finalized? Are all areas that you consider important scheduled to be assessed (so you get the most out of the assessment)?

Continued on next page

Procedures	❑ Are all standard operating procedures current with the quality manual policies and requirements?
	❑ Are procedures in all areas of the proper revision? Is the control of procedure revisions well understood by all personnel (and adhered to)?
Training	❑ Do all employees understand the quality policy and objectives for quality? The quality manual and systems that affect them?
	❑ Are all records for this training current?
	❑ Have all senior managers from areas to be visited been briefed on the assessment? Line personnel?
Procedural Documentation	❑ Is there documentation in all areas of the assessment?
	❑ Are the records complete and up to date? Do they reflect the procedural requirements that created them?
Assessment Documentation	❑ Has an assessment coordinator been appointed?
	❑ Will someone be available to take complete notes during the assessment?
Daily Briefings	❑ Have you arranged for daily debriefings of each day's assessment activities? (This is an opportunity to take immediate corrective action or minor observations.)

Adapted from a paper presented by Dr. Steve Wirkus, Advanced Cardiovascular Systems, Inc., Temecula, CA, at the ASQC 49th Annual Quality Congress. (The American Society for Quality Control, Inc., 1995. Reprinted with permission.)

Lessons Learned in Implementing ISO 9001

- Obtain support from upper management.
- Manage ISO 9000 as a company-wide project.
- Set individual management goals and evaluate them periodically.
- Budget resources in advance.
- Be selective in choosing your registrar.
- Adopt ISO 9000 by using a cross-functional team approach (not just a quality assurance department task group).
- Benchmark a company that is registered.
- Flowchart all activities, not just production activities.
- Develop a training matrix.
- Take time to celebrate along the way.

Experience of Haworth, Inc. Holland, MI, as related by William J. Vance, Quality Systems Manager

More Lessons Learned

- Communicate early and often with everyone.
- Develop a rapport with your registrar.
- Pay attention to the details.
- Develop well-written procedures. Make sure people are trained on writing effective specifications.
- Continually look for ways to simplify and improve your work.

Chapter 3

The ISO 9001 Standard

ISO 9001 Quality Systems Standard/ QS-9000 Requirements

The ISO 9001 Quality Systems Standard and QS-9000 Requirements describe what you and your organization must do to assure your customer or "third-party" registrar that you have an effective quality management system in place. Taken individually, there are 20 clauses that describe these requirements. However, taken as a whole, the ISO 9001 Quality Assurance Model defines three basic areas: administration and control of your quality system; the steps to realizing your product or service; and the necessary support activities.

The following section describes the contents of ISO 9001 and also summarizes QS-9000 requirements. The subclauses to QS-9000 are starred (*) and in **bold type** on the first page of each ISO 9001 clause. The subclauses are further expanded in the section **"What else do I need to meet QS-9000?"**

Note: *The wording for ISO 9001 and QS-9000 has been paraphrased in this chapter. An effort has been made* **not to change the meaning** *of the requirements of the standard. For actual phrasing, please refer to the texts of ISO 9001 and QS-9000, as well as ISO 9000-2 "Generic Guidelines for the Application of ISO 9001."*

ISO 9001 Quality Assurance Model

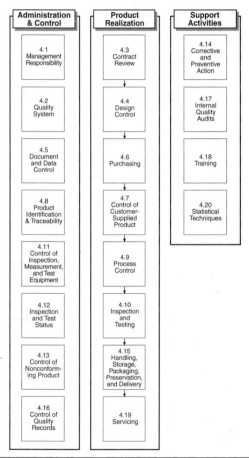

Administration & Control

- 4.1 Management Responsibility
- 4.2 Quality System
- 4.5 Document and Data Control
- 4.8 Product Identification & Traceability
- 4.11 Control of Inspection, Measurement, and Test Equipment
- 4.12 Inspection and Test Status
- 4.13 Control of Nonconforming Product
- 4.16 Control of Quality Records

Product Realization

- 4.3 Contract Review
- 4.4 Design Control
- 4.6 Purchasing
- 4.7 Control of Customer-Supplied Product
- 4.9 Process Control
- 4.10 Inspection and Testing
- 4.15 Handling, Storage, Packaging, Preservation, and Delivery
- 4.19 Servicing

Support Activities

- 4.14 Corrective and Preventive Action
- 4.17 Internal Quality Audits
- 4.18 Training
- 4.20 Statistical Techniques

4.1 Management Responsibility

4.1.1 Quality Policy
4.1.2 Organization
    * **Organizational Interfaces**
4.1.2.1 Responsibility and Authority
4.1.2.2 Resources
4.1.2.3 Management Representative
*4.1.3 **Management Review**
*4.1.4 **Business Plan**
*4.1.5 **Analysis and Use of Company-Level Data**
*4.1.6 **Customer Satisfaction**
                *QS-9000 Requirements

Why do it?

To make certain that executive management takes a leading and visible role in defining, implementing, and administering the quality system, with the goal of meeting all customer requirements.

What is it?

An orderly documentation of executive management's responsibilities in establishing, reviewing, and providing resources to support the company's quality system.

How do I do it?

1. **Establish a quality policy.**
   - Assign responsibility to an individual or team to develop the quality policy. It should include:
     - The organization's quality objectives
     - Management's commitment to quality
     - Relevance to organizational goals
     - Expectations and needs of customers
   - Ask for input from across the company to ensure "ownership" of the quality policy.
   - Develop comprehensive objectives.
   - Consider organizational goals.

2. **Develop a plan to ensure that the policy is understood, implemented, and maintained at all levels.**
   • Conduct an orientation for new employees.
   • Display copies of the policy.
   • Hold departmental meetings/discussions.
   • Reinforce and follow-up on the ideas in the policy.
   • Verify that awareness and understanding is uniform.

3. **Define responsibility, authority, and how the assignments are interrelated.**
   • Prepare organizational charts.
   • Review and expand job descriptions for those whose work affects quality and who have authority over the following:
     - Identifying problems
     - Generating solutions
     - Initiating corrective action to avoid recurrence of the problems
     - Verifying implementation of the corrective action
     - Controlling nonconforming product

4. **Identify resource requirements.**
   • Provide resources and assign trained personnel for:
     - Management
     - Work performance
     - Verification activities

5. **Appoint a management representative who:**
   • Ensures that the quality system is established and implemented
   • Reports on the performance of the quality system

6. **Provide for management review of the quality system.**
   • Assess quality audit results.
   • Ensure suitability and effectiveness in meeting policy and objectives.
   • Maintain records.

Controlled Documents Needed

- Quality Policy: a statement of your organization's objectives, (identified and monitored), and commitment to quality
- Clear assignment of individual responsibility, lines of authority, and interrelation of all personnel whose work affects quality. Special concern to be given to duties of personnel assigned to:
  - Initiate preventive action
  - Identify and recommend solutions to problems
  - Verify implementation of correction
  - Control further production and distribution activities until problem is corrected
- Record of resource requirements and in-house verification activities
- Management review procedures

Quality Records Needed

- Dissemination of quality policy, for understanding, implementation, and maintenance
- Management review activities, including corrective action taken

---

What else do I need to meet QS-9000?

*4.1.2 Organizational Interfaces

- Systems are to be in place during advanced planning stages. (See *Advanced Product Quality and Control Plan* Reference Manual, p. 157.)
- Use multi-discipline approach to decision making.
- Communicate information and data in customer-prescribed format.

Continued on next page

*4.1.3 Management Review
• Shall include all elements of the quality system

*4.1.4 Business Plan
• The plan should cover short term (1-2 years) and longer term (3+ years) and include:
  - Competitive analysis and benchmarking
  - How to determine customer expectations
  - Use of a valid information collection process
  - Documented procedures to assure use of plan
  - Data-driven process improvement
  - How employees will be empowered

Note: *Contents of the business plan are not subject to third-party audit.*

*4.1.5 Analysis and Use of Company-Level Data
• Document quality and performance trends.
• Compare your data to competitors and/or appropriate benchmarks.
• Take action to solve customer-related problems.
• Support status review, decision making and long-term planning.

*4.1.6 Customer Satisfaction
• Document the process for determining the frequency, objectivity, and validity of customer satisfaction.
• Document trends and key indicators of dissatisfaction.
• Compare trends to competition and benchmarks.
• Senior management should review trends.
• Consider both immediate and final customers.

Pitfalls

4.1.1 Quality Policy

- No policy statement exists.
- A policy statement is written, but not understood or implemented at all levels, particularly at the shop floor level.
- Objectives are not clearly defined.

4.1.2.1 Responsibility and Authority

- Managers have no written statement of their responsibilities, authority, and accountability.
- Managers are not implementing their responsibility and authority.
- Where an organization chart is used, there is no back-up information on the systems or interfaces.
- Interfaces and relationships between departments and personnel do not exist or are not defined.

4.1.2.2 Resources

- There is a lack of adequate resources.
- There is a lack of trained personnel. (The organization lays down required training, but does not follow its own rules.)
- Internal audits are not being carried out by a person independent of the person having direct responsibility for the area.
- There are no relationships/interfaces, particularly with feedback from installation and servicing.

Continued on next pag

4.1.2.3 Management Representative

- The management representative has inadequately defined responsibilities and authority.

- The management representative is not implementing his/her defined responsibilities and authority.

4.1.3 Management Review

- No review system exists.

- Corrective action on internal audit results has not been carried out.

Guidance in Preparing the Quality Policy

(Based on ISO 9000-2 and ISO 9004-1)

- Make it easy to understand.
- Make it ambitious, yet achievable.
- Relate objectives to performance (including quality goals), fitness for use, safety, and reliability.
- Consider costs to minimize losses.
- Establish quality objectives at appropriate levels of management.
- Provide sufficient resources to reach the objectives.
- Determine and provide the necessary training.
- Control all activities that affect quality.
- Emphasize prevention.
- Indicate the method to be used and the criteria to be met.

4.2 Quality System

4.2.1 General
4.2.2 Quality System Procedures
4.2.3 Quality Planning
* **Quality Planning**
* **Special Characteristics**
* **Use of Cross-Functional Teams**
* **Feasibility Reviews**
* **Process Failure Mode and Effects Analysis (Process FMEAs)**
* **The Control Plan**

*QS-9000 Requirements

Why do it?

To make certain that your quality practices provide product and services that meet your customer needs and will continue to do so consistently in the future.

What is it?

A means to demonstrate, through documented procedures, that:

- The quality system is in support of a quality manual that refers to procedures and instructions.
- A quality plan is in operation.
- The overall system is in effective use.

How do I do it?

1. **Determine the requirements of the standard, including both documentation and implementation.**

2. **Determine which ISO 9000 standard applies (9001, 9002, or 9003).**

3. **Plan the structure of the documentation:**
   - Quality manual (Refer to ANSI/ISO/ASQC Q 10013:1995, "Guidelines for Developing Quality Manuals.")

A typical outline includes:
- Quality policy
- Organizational chart
- Quality assurance organization
- Statement of authority and responsibility
- Distribution list of controlled copies
- Quality system: clauses 4.1–4.20
- Procedures index
- Forms index
- Operating procedures
- Job instructions
- Records, forms, and specifications

4. Establish existing company practices by using:
- Flowcharts
- Procedures (written and unwritten)
- Work/job instructions

5. Evaluate resources, present and needed.
- Personnel
- Equipment and instrumentation
- Specifications and acceptance standards
- Quality records

6. Establish a quality planning function to meet requirements for:
- Products
- Projects
- Contracts

7. Implement the quality system. Consider:
- Quality plans
- Needed resources/time frames
- Updating procedures and instrumentation
- Identifying extreme measurement requirements
- Clarifying acceptance standards
- Compatible elements
- Quality records

Controlled Documents Needed
- Quality plans
- Quality manual
- Operating procedures
- Work/job instructions

Quality Records Needed
- Quality records specified in documentation procedures

What else do I need to meet QS-9000?

*4.2.3 Quality Planning
Use the *Advanced Product Quality Planning and Control Plan* Reference Manual (see Chapter 5, page 157) for:
- Planning
- Product design and development
- Process design and development
- Product and process validation
- Production
- Feedback assessment and corrective action

*Special Characteristics
Establish appropriate process controls for special characteristics.

*Use of Cross-Functional Teams
Internal cross-functional teams are to use techniques in the *Advanced Product Quality Planning and Control Plan* Reference Manual (see Chapter 5, p. 157).

*Feasibility Reviews
Confirm manufacturing feasibility prior to contracting.

Continued on next pag

©1996 GOAL/QP(

*Process FMEAs

Improve processes to prevent rather than detect defects, using techniques in the *Potential Failure Modes and Effects* Reference Manual (see Chapter 5, p. 157).

*The Control Plan

Develop Control Plans—the output of the advanced quality planning process—for:
- Prototype (may not be required from all suppliers)
- Pre-launch
- Production

Pitfalls

- The quality system is incomplete.
- The quality system is not adequately documented.
- The quality manual is not complete, or only "paper systems" exist.
- There are faults in the system, e.g., unauthorized changes to documents.
- There is a lack of a quality plan for a specific product/project which requires a deviation/addition to the normal procedures contained in the quality manual.
- Inspection procedures are insufficient.
- Testing methods are incorrect.
- Subjective elements are being used when a specific one is available.
- Too much design is taking place with no involvement of production, and this is causing production to deviate from an impossible-to-achieve specification.
- Records are inadequate.

4.2 Quality System

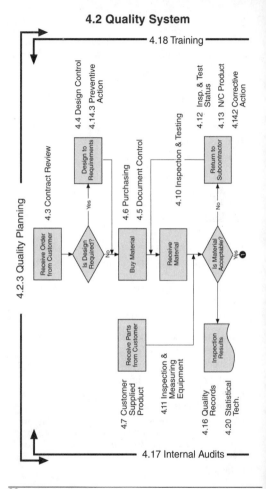

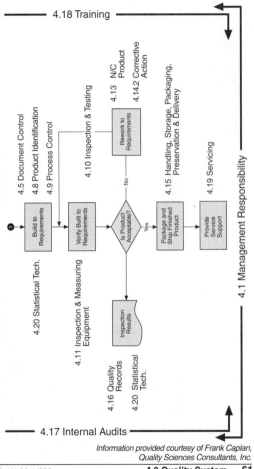

Information provided courtesy of Frank Caplan,
Quality Sciences Consultants, Inc.

Partial Example of a Format of a Quality Plan for a Processed Material

Part	Process Flowchart	Process Stage	Work Instruction Number	Quality characteristic to be controlled (Process condition to be checked)	Instruction for Process Control Number	Control Method	Responsible Function	Verification/ Instruction	Parameters	Procedure Number
							Work-station			
Part A		Pre-heating	WI-123	Temp-erature	IPC-22	Check Sheet Ref. No. 1	A	VI-29		
		Forming	WI-321	Temp-erature, pressure		Check Sheet Ref. No. 2	B			
		Cutting		Length			C			
				Measure length		Control Chart Ref. No. 1	D			
				Yield					Length	IT-5

Column groups: **Process Control** covers Instruction for Process Control Number, Control Method, Responsible Function, Verification/Instruction. **Inspection** covers Parameters, Procedure Number.

Symbol Key: Manufacturing ● / Inspection and testing ◇ / Storage ▽

BSR/ANSI/ISO/ASQC Q 10005

Quality Plan for Service Calls

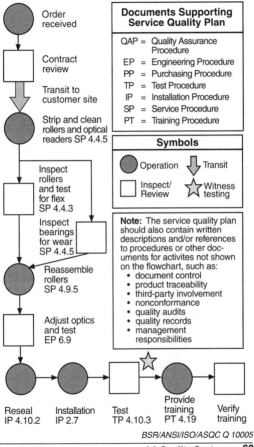

Order received

Contract review

Transit to customer site

Strip and clean rollers and optical readers SP 4.4.5

Inspect rollers and test for flex SP 4.4.3

Inspect bearings for wear SP 4.4.5

Reassemble rollers SP 4.9.5

Adjust optics and test EP 6.9

Reseal IP 4.10.2

Installation IP 2.7

Test TP 4.10.3

Provide training PT 4.19

Verify training

Documents Supporting Service Quality Plan

QAP = Quality Assurance Procedure
EP = Engineering Procedure
PP = Purchasing Procedure
TP = Test Procedure
IP = Installation Procedure
SP = Service Procedure
PT = Training Procedure

Symbols

Operation
Transit
Inspect/Review
Witness testing

Note: The service quality plan should also contain written descriptions and/or references to procedures or other documents for activites not shown on the flowchart, such as:
- document control
- product traceability
- third-party involvement
- nonconformance
- quality audits
- quality records
- management responsibilities

BSR/ANSI/ISO/ASQC Q 10005

Sample Format
(To use in writing either a section of a quality manual
or describing a quality system procedure.)

Organization		Title/Subject		Number	
Unit Issuing	Approved by		Date	Revision	Page

Policy/Policy Reference
State the governing requirement.

Purpose and Scope
State why the document or procedure is used or what it
accomplishes, the area it covers, and any exclusions
or exceptions.

Responsibility
Identify the organizational unit or units responsible
for implementing the document which will achieve the
purpose.

Action/Method to Achieve System Element Requirement.
List the details, step by step, of what needs to be
done. Use references if appropriate. Put the list of
items in a logical sequence. Mention any exceptions or
specific areas of attention.

Documentation/References
Identify which referenced documents or forms are
associated with using the document, or what data have
to be recorded. Use examples, if appropriate.

Records
Identify which records are generated as a result of
using the document, where these records are retained,
and the length of time they are retained.

ANSI/ISO/ASQC Q 10013:1995, p. 14

Note 1: The structure and order of the items you choose to use in
your documentation format should be based on your own
organizational needs.

Note 2: Approval and revision status should be identified on the
documentation.

4.3 Contract Review

4.3.1 General
*4.3.2 Review
4.3.3 Amendment to a Contract
4.3.4 Records

*QS-9000 Requirements

Why do it?

To make certain that you will be able to meet your customers' needs before accepting an order.

What is it?

Documentation that you understand customer needs, and are sure that all requirements are adequately defined, and that requirements that differ from those in the *"tender"* or *"contract"* are resolved. You are to be following a procedure for reviewing requests for quotations, contracts, or accepted orders.

- *"Tender"* is an offer made to a supplier in response to an invitation to satisfy a contract award to provide product.

- *"Contract"* is an agreed requirement between a supplier and customer, transmitted by any means.

How do I do it?

1. **Document the customer's requirements.**

2. **Identify pre-contract practice.**

3. **Establish contract review procedures.**

4. **Verify the capability to meet requirements.**

5. **Internalize customer's requirements and resolve any differences.**

6. Maintain control of customer purchase orders that are written under one contract.

7. Develop a plan for deployment.

8. Establish customer purchase order review procedures.

9. Obtain customer agreements.

10. Revise/improve procedures .

11. Evaluate revisions.

Controlled Documents Needed
- Procedures for reviewing contracts
- Product and service specifications
- Contract or accepted customer order

Quality Records Needed
- Evidence of ability to meet contract requirements
- Proof of contract review
- Resolution of deviations from contract

What else do I need to meet QS-9000?

*4.3.2 Review
Review tender, contract or order before submission, to assure that all customer requirements, including QS-9000 Section III, Customer-specific Requirements, can be met.

Pitfalls

- No contract procedures exist.

- Procedures are incomplete, misunderstood (often deliberately), or contradict each other, e.g., design vs. sales vs. production.

- Records are inadequate or don't exist.

- There is a lack of customer involvement.

- There is no documented procedure for handling verbal orders.

Contract Review Process

(Based on ISO 9000-2)

Process steps include:

- Give all affected parties the opportunity to review the contract.
- Use a checklist to verify all contract elements are included.
- Provide for a way to make changes in the contract.
- Reach agreement.
- Discuss the results of the contract review.
- Discuss the quality plan draft.

What to consider in the contract:

- Reference to product specifications

Continued on next page

- Delivery information
  - Dates
  - Location
  - Method of transit
  - Packing
  - Product identification
  - Carton marking
- Responsibilities for
  - Nonconforming product
  - Product quality verification
  - Contract review
  - Resolution of differences
- A service provider list might contain:
  - Performance criteria
  - Costs

©1996 GOAL/QPC

4.4 Design Control

Why do it?

To make certain that the product you produce meets all specified design requirements set by the customer and regulatory agencies.

What is it?

Procedures to control, verify, and validate product design and supporting software. A design control process in operation that has adequate resources and assigned responsibilities.

How do I do it?

1. Document all customer requirements and any other pertinent requirements (input).

2. Establish a plan for design control and assign responsibilities.

3. Assign qualified staff; provide adequate resources.

4. Obtain input from all cross-functional activities to establish interfaces.

5. **Document the control procedures, with milestones required by the standard.**

6. **Design output to do the following:**
   - Meet input requirements
   - Contain reference data
   - Meet regulations
   - Consider safety
   - Review documentation before release

7. **Provide output verification through the following:**
   - Alternative calculations
   - Comparison with proven design
   - Qualification tests
   - Review of documents before release

8. **Validate the design.**
   - Ensure that design verification is successful
   - Confirm that the final product meets user needs
   - Assess the need for multiple validations

9. **Develop change control procedures.**
   - Identification
   - Documentation
   - Review
   - Approval

Controlled Documents Needed
   - Documentation of procedures, responsibilities, and resources for:
     - Design input and design output
     - Design review
     - Design verification
     - Design validation
     - Design changes

Quality Records Needed

- Group interface communications
- Design input approval
- Design output verification
- Design review findings
- Design verification results
- Design validation results
- Design change approval

What else do I need to meet QS-9000?

*4.4.2 Required Skills

As appropriate, design personnel are to have specific required skills:

- Geometric Dimensioning and Tolerancing (GD&T)
- Quality Function Deployment (QFD)
- Design for Manufacturing (DFM)/Design for Assembly (DFA)
- Value Engineering (VE)
- Design of Experiments (Taguchi and classical)
- Failure Mode and Effects Analysis (DFMEA/PFMEA, etc.)
- Finite Element Analysis (FEA)
- Solid modeling
- Simulation techniques
- Computer-Aided Design (CAD)/Computer-Aided Engineering (CAE)
- Reliability engineering plans

QS-9000 Quality System Requirement

*4.4.4 Design Input–Supplemental

Appropriate resources for computer-aided product design, engineering and analysis (CAD/CAE).

Continued on next page

*4.4.5 Design Output–Supplemental

Evaluation to include:

- Simplification, optimization, innovation, waste reduction, and environmental concerns
- Geometric dimensioning and tolerancing
- Cost/performance/risk analysis
- Feedback from testing, production, and field
- Design FMEAs

*4.4.7 Design Verification–Supplemental

- Prototype program (unless waived)
- Use the same subcontractors, tooling, and processes whenever possible
- Test life, reliability, and durability
- Track completion of performance tests
- Services may be subcontracted

*4.4.9 Design Changes–Supplemental

Customer must approve all design changes for impact on form, fit, function, performance, and durability.

Pitfalls

- Design responsibilities/authorities/interfaces are not specified in writing, or not followed.
- Drawings are not under control:
  - Irrational tolerances
  - Not checked or verified
  - Not authorized or no use of a change control system
  - Subjective descriptions on drawings

Continued on next page

- There is a lack of real design reviews, e.g., system operated by one person (individual invites participants by choice).
- A system exists but is not being used.
- The tolerances that are specified are impossible to achieve, e.g., lack of production involvement.
- Prototypes are not subjected to critical examination.
- User publication requirements are not started until design is almost complete.
- Gauges and test equipment on experimental work are not calibrated.
- Sampling systems are faulty or not agreed to by the customer.

Stages in the Design Control Process

Stage	What is required?
Design Planning	• Procedures for each activity • Responsibilities identified • Resources adequate; qualified resources • Interfaces between groups defined • Communication between groups established • Plans updated as design evolves

Design Input	• Design requirements identified, including:
	  - Acceptance criteria
	  - Requirements of regulatory bodies
	  - Proper functioning
	  - Safety characteristics
	• Reviewed for adequacy
	• Incomplete, ambiguous or conflicting requirements resolved

Continued on next page

Stage	What is required?
Design Output	• Technical documents to be used from production through servicing (drawings, specifications, instructions and procedures) that are crucial to safe functioning of the product, including operation, storage, handling, maintenance, and disposal • Output documents to be reviewed before release
Design Review	• Scheduled reviews of development status with all participating groups • Record of reviews maintained
Design Verification	A plan to verify that output meets input. Techniques may include: • Alternative calculations • Comparison to other designs • Tests and demonstrations • Document review
Design Validation	A plan to validate that user needs and requirements are met • Follows successful verification • Defined operating conditions • Normally done on final product • May have different validations for specific intended uses
Design Change	A plan to control design changes before implementation • Identify • Document • Review • Approve

The difference between verification and validation:
- Verification compares design output to input; it is the *producer's* point of view.
- Validation ensures that the product meets user needs and requirements; it is the *customer's* point of view.

4.5 Document and Data Control

Why do it?

To make certain that quality system documents and data are controlled so that they are readily available to all users when they need them.

What is it?

A method for establishing and maintaining procedures to ensure that documents and data are:

- Accessible
- Updated (with obsolete documents properly dealt with)
- Reviewed and revised periodically
- Controlled with hard copy, electronic or other media

How do I do it?

1. **List all documents.**

2. **Establish a plan to administer each category of document.**
   - Document original procedures.
   - Verify review and approval of documents.
   - Consider the pros and cons of hard copy versus electronic media.

3. **Investigate conformity to the plan.**

4. **Ensure accessibility at the work/job site.** Accessibility includes:
   - A document master list or reference index of all documents
   - Organization of documents and data in a way that makes them available to those using them
   - Formatting documents to provide ready access to information
   - Removal of obsolete documents

5. **Establish control over documents that become obsolete.**

6. **Establish/implement change control procedures.**
   - Changes to documents are to be reviewed and approved by the same process followed for original documents
   - Those functions approving changes are to have background information on which to base their review and approval
   - When changes are made, the nature of the change should be identified on the document, as appropriate

7. **Investigate conformity to change procedures.**

Controlled Documents Needed
   - Procedures for documents and data approval and data control
   - Master list of documents and data sheets
   - A schedule for review of documents and data

Quality Records Needed
   - Results of document and data reviews
   - Distribution lists
   - Identification on documents of nature of change

*4.5.1 Reference Documents
Specific types of documents to be included in document control, as follows:

- Engineering drawings
- Engineering standards
- Math (CAD) data
- Inspection instructions
- Test procedures
- Work instructions
- Operations sheets
- Quality manual
- Operational procedures
- Quality assurance procedures
- Material specifications
                    QS-9000 Quality System Requirement

*Document Identification for Special Characteristics
Special requirements by the customer should be separately identified by the customer's special characteristic symbol.

*4.5.2 Engineering Specifications
A procedure is to be established for timely review (days, not weeks or months) of all standards and specification changes, with a record of implementation date.

Pitfalls

- No real control system exists.
- No person has been assigned responsibility.
- There is no disciplined recall system for obsolete or modified documents.
- Work/job instructions are not at the place of work.
- There are unauthorized changes in documents.
- Changes are not made to all issues of documents.
- There are pencilled changes.
- Changes are not verified with the function that issued the document.

Types of Quality Documents that Require Control

(Guidance from ISO 9004-1)

Quality Documents (*What you are asked to do*)
- Drawings
- Specifications
- Inspection procedures and instructions
- Test procedures
- Work instructions
- Operation sheets
- Quality manual and quality plans
- Operational procedures
- Quality system procedures

Examples of quality documents:
- Procedures for document control, page 21
- Work/job instruction, page 23

Note: *The record of what you have done is required in 4.16.*

Sample Controlled Document

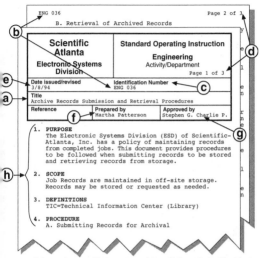

Information provided courtesy of Sam Tolbert, Scientific Atlanta

A "controlled document" will have:

(a) Title

(b) Document number: a unique identifier

(c) Revision indicator (e.g., Rev. A, -001, [blank] in this case it is blank)

(d) Page number (e.g., Page 1 of 3, Page 1.2, 1-2.3)

(e) Date issued/revised (e.g., April 6, 1996, 4/6/96)

(f) Prepared by/Issued by (name, position, and/or department)

(g) Approval (the approving authority by signature and perhaps also position title)

(h) Document Content

Example of a Quality Document

Part No. _____
Part Name _____
Sampling Reference _____
Prepared by _____

Supplier Name _____
Laboratory Required _____ No. _____
Equipment No. _____ Line No. _____

Revisions
Approved by _____ Date _____

Part Sketch

Operation No.	Char. No.	C/C*	Characteristic Description	Limits	Sample Size	Inspection Equipment/Method	Equipment Numbers

*Characteristic Classification   C – Critical   M – Major   N – Minor   I = Incidental

*Provided by Frank Caplan, Quality Sciences Consultants, Inc.
Developed as an exhibit for* The Quality System: A Sourcebook for *Managers and Engineers, by Frank Caplan, Chilton Book Co., 1990.*

4.6 Purchasing

Why do it?

To make certain the product received from your subcontractors meets your requirements. You, in turn, incorporate this product into your production process to make the product that meets your customer's requirements. "Product" includes hardware, software, processed material, and service.

What is it?

A means to demonstrate effective operation of procedures for the purchasing process, which would include, as appropriate:
- Subcontractor evaluation
- Purchasing data
- Verification of purchased product

Reminder: those who provide services are subcontractors, as well, e.g., freight carriers, outside calibration services.

How do I do it?

1. **Evaluate existing purchasing specifications and requirements.**
   - Review the process for developing and approving specifications.
   - Update the procedures, if necessary.

2. **Begin upgrading specifications as required.**
   • Prioritize criticality in meeting requirements.

3. **Prepare, review, and approve purchasing documents.**
   • Refer to the updated specifications.

4. **Establish criteria for determining subcontractor acceptability.**
   • Evaluate and select subcontractors based on their ability to meet requirements, including:
     - Product requirements (What is the subcontractor's product quality history?)
     - Delivery dependability
     - Quality system capability (via audit/ISO 9000)

5. **Develop a subcontractor classification system.**
   • Start with a list of acceptable subcontractors.
   • Define the extent of control to be exercised over subcontractors based on:
     - Type of product
     - Impact on final product quality
     - Results of previous quality audits
     - Previously demonstrated quality capability
   • A qualified supplier list should include:
     - Raw materials
     - Tooling
     - Equipment
     - Business service providers such as consultants and registrars (auditors)

6. **Establish a record system.**
   Keep records on the following:
   • Subcontractor's quality capability
   • Established procedures for communicating requirements and performance with subcontractors
   • Results of periodic subcontractor review
   • Purchase contracts and supporting data
   • Review and approval of purchasing data

7. **Deploy the plan through the following:**
   - Develop a schedule
   - Coordinate with receiving inspection
   - Assign responsibility for administration

8. **Revise/improve procedures.**

9. **Evaluate revisions.**

Controlled Documents Needed
   - Purchasing procedures
   - Product specifications
   - List of acceptable subcontractors

Quality Records Needed
   - Subcontractor selection, including assessment of the subcontractor's capability and the effectiveness of the quality system
   - Established procedures for communicating requirements and performance with subcontractors, e.g., written documents, periodic visits, meetings
   - Results of periodic subcontractor review
   - Purchase contracts and supporting data
   - Review and approval of purchasing data

What else do I need to meet QS-9000?

*4.6.1 Approved Materials for Ongoing Production
When required, the supplier (your organization) may purchase material from subcontractors that have been approved by the customer.

*4.6.2 Subcontractor Development
The supplier will perform subcontractor quality system development.

Continued on next page

Subcontractor assessment options include audit by:
- Supplier, in accordance with ISO 9001/QS-9000
- Customer-approved OEM second-party
- Accredited third-party registrar

Note: *Responsibility for ensuring quality always remains with the supplier.*

*Scheduling Subcontractors
- 100% on-time delivery performance required of subcontractors
- Supplier to plan and commit accordingly
- Subcontractor delivery performance and premium freight costs to be monitored

*4.6.3 Restricted Substances
The subcontractor is to provide materials that satisfy government requirements for:
- Restricted, toxic, and hazardous materials
- Environmental factors
- Electrical and electromagnetic requirements

The supplier is to have a process to assure compliance with these requirements.

Pitfalls

- There is a lack of control or no evidence of control of subcontractors.
- There are no records of acceptable subcontractors.
- You violate the rule of "We only buy from approved subcontractors."
- There is insufficient data on purchasing documents.
- You do not inform subcontractors of the requirement of 4.6.4 when formalizing contracts.
- You do not follow your own systems, e.g., a telephone order that has no written confirmation.

Typical Content of Purchase Orders

- (A) Quantity
- (B) Identification and description of the product
- (C) Cost information
- (D) Billing instructions
- (E) Shipping instructions
- (F) Packing instructions
- (G) Requirements for approval of product, process, or personnel
- (H) The appropriate ISO 9000 standard to be applied
- (I) Requirements for product verification and release to the subcontractor

PURCHASE ORDER

Bill To: (D)

Ship To: (E)

Quantity	Part #	Description	Cost/unit	Total Cost
(A)	(B)	(B)	(C)	(C)

Additional Comments: (F) (G) (H) (I)

4.7 Control of Customer-Supplied Product

Why do it?

To make certain that the product you receive from your customers will be incorporated into your product and ultimately meet all of your customers' requirements.

What is it?

Documented procedures for verification, storage, and maintenance of customer-supplied product.

How do I do it?

1. Determine the existence of customer-supplied product (including test equipment).

2. Document the existing practice for:
   • Verification
   • Storage
   • Maintenance

3. Revise/improve your procedures.

4. Evaluate revisions.

Controlled Documents Needed
- Procedures for verification process
- Procedures for storage process
- Procedures for maintenance process
- Procedures for controlling nonconformances

Quality Records Needed
- Receipt and verification results
- Rejected product, (lost, damaged, unusable)
- Product inventory records
- Reports to customer

What else do I need to meet QS-9000?

Includes customer-owned tooling and returnable packaging.

Pitfalls
- Items are damaged or stored badly.
- Customer-supplied product is not identified adequately.

Customer-Supplied Product

This is product owned by the *customer*, which is provided to the supplier (you), to be incorporated into your product. Your customer, in this case, serves as your subcontractor. Examples:

- Customer labels or logo emblems for attachment to your product or customer packaging furnished for your product
- Printed instructions and/or accessories for inclusion with your cartoned product
- Tooling provided by your customer
- Test and inspection equipment provided by your customer, for your use in product verification or validation
- A service, such as your use of your customer's delivery service

4.8 Product Identification and Traceability

Why do it?

To make certain that your product is properly identified at all stages of production, and to avoid errors that can cause scrap and rework.

What is it?

A provision for identifying incoming materials, in-process product, and finished product. Where required, it is a record that tracks the history, usage, and location of product.

- *Identification:* The ability to separate two or more materials or products.
- *Traceability:* The ability to separate material or product by individual unit, batch, lot, or run.

How do I do it?

1. Establish customer and/or regulatory requirements.

2. Document existing traceability practices, to include the following:
   - From your subcontractor
   - In your plant
   - To your customer
   - At/after installation

3. Revise/improve traceability procedures.

4. **Consider types of traceability/identification:**
   - Unit identification (serial number)
   - Lot identification
   - Production date code

5. **Consider methods of identification:**
   - Paper versus electronic
   - Labeling
   - Bar codes

6. **Determine the following about the records to be kept:**
   - Availability
   - Retention times
   - Responsibility

Controlled Documents Needed

- Procedures for product and lot identification at all stages, such as:
  - Receiving activity
  - Production
  - Final product acceptance
  - Warehousing and distribution
- Product lists

Quality Records Needed

- Material batches, lots or units at all stages, such as:
  - Receiving
  - Production
  - Final product acceptance
  - Warehousing and distribution

©1996 GOAL/QPC

What else do I need to meet QS-9000?

For QS-9000 Requirements, "Where appropriate" refers to situations where product identity is not inherently obvious.

Pitfalls

- Components, materials, or products are unmarked.
- Batches are stacked on top of each other, when batch identity is required.
- A stage or operation is missing, when traceability is necessary.

Identification vs. Traceability

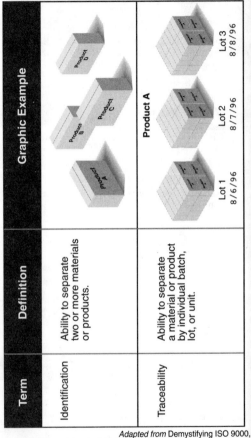

Term	Definition	Graphic Example
Identification	Ability to separate two or more materials or products.	Product A, Product B, Product C, Product D
Traceability	Ability to separate a material or product by individual batch, lot, or unit.	Product A — Lot 1 8/6/96, Lot 2 8/7/96, Lot 3 8/8/96

Adapted from Demystifying ISO 9000,
Information Mapping's Guide to the ISO 9000 Standards, *p. 2-32*

4.9 Process Control

* Government Safety and Environmental Regulations
* Designation of Special Characteristics
* Preventive Maintenance
*4.9.1 Process Monitoring and Operator Instructions
*4.9.2 Preliminary Process Capability Requirements
*4.9.3 Ongoing Process Performance Requirements
*4.9.4 Modified Preliminary or Ongoing Capability Requirements
*4.9.5 Verification of Job Set-Ups
*4.9.6 Process Changes
*4.9.7 Appearance Items

*QS-9000 Requirements

Why do it?

To make certain that all of your processes (production, installation, and servicing) are carried out under controlled conditions to minimize variability in the manufacture of product or service.

What is it?

Documented procedures for your processes (production, installation, and servicing), that:

- Identify and plan the steps to produce/deliver the product or service
- Ensure equipment is suitable and operated under controlled conditions
- Ensure suitable working environment
- Prepare documented instructions for all activities affecting quality
- Monitor and approve processes
- Establish workmanship criteria as needed
- Maintain equipment to ensure process capability

How do I do it?

1. Base process control on the quality plan.

2. Identify critical control points.

3. Define factors affecting key processes controls (production, installation, and service):
   • Equipment
   • Work environment
   • Hazardous material control

4. Identify the following product requirements:
   • Specifications
   • Workmanship standards
   • Regulatory standards and codes

5. Review existing monitoring techniques.

6. Develop control and approval procedures.

7. Develop work/job instructions.
   See "Level 3: Preparing Work/Job Instructions," page 22.

8. Develop control equipment maintenance procedures.
   See "Level 2: Preparing Quality Procedures," page 18.

9. Identify special processes.

10. Implement process change control.
    Refer to *The Memory Jogger™ II*, page 25, "Improving Work Processes," and the Customer Reference Manuals listed on page 157.

11. Revise/improve procedures.

12. Evaluate revisions.

Controlled Documents Needed

- Quality Plan
- Procedures for:
  - Product control
  - Monitoring
  - Change approval
  - Maintenance
- Reference standards and codes (health, safety, environment)
- Product standards representative samples, and illustrations, as appropriate
- Work/job instructions

Quality Records Needed

- Process change approvals
- Special process approvals of equipment and personnel
- Process monitoring results
- Process maintenance

What else do I need to meet QS-9000?

*Government Safety and Environmental Regulations
You are to have processes to ensure that applicable regulations, including those on hazardous materials, are met. Where appropriate, have certificates or letters of compliance.

*Designation of Special Characteristics
Documentation is required to show that you are meeting specific customer requirements. "Special" characteristics may affect safety, regulation compliance, fit, function, appearance, or effect on later manufacturing operations.

Continued on next page

*Preventive Maintenance

You will develop a planned preventive maintenance system requiring:

- Procedures
- Predictive maintenance
- Schedule
- Replacement parts

*4.9.1 Process Monitoring and Operation Instructions

You will need to develop and maintain explicit instructions called for in the *Advanced Product Quality Planning and Control Plan* Reference Manual. Your instructions are to include, as appropriate:

- Operation name and number keyed to a process flowchart (see "Flowcharting a Process," page 27.)
- Part name and part number
- Current engineering level/date
- Required tools, gauges, and other equipment
- Material identification and disposition instructions
- Customer/supplier designated special characteristics
- SPC requirements
- Relevant engineering and manufacturing standards
- Inspection and test instructions (4.10.4)
- Corrective action instructions
- Revision date and approvals
- Visual aids
- Tool change intervals and set-up instructions

  QS-9000 Quality System Requirement

*4.9.2 Preliminary Process Capability Requirements

- Studies are required for new processes, to meet customer requirements. If no requirements are specified, then a P_{pk} target of 1.67 should be achieved. (See "Mistake proofing" on p. 139, and the *Production Part Approval Process* Reference Manual. For other techniques, see "Continuous Improvement" on p. 138.)

- Statement on limitation of use of attributes data.

*4.9.3 Ongoing Process Performance Requirements
- C_{pk} 1.33 target for stable processes
- P_{pk} 1.67 target for unstable processes that meet specification and have a predictable pattern
- Note significant changes on control charts
- Customer can permit revision of Control Plan when high degree of process capability is indicated
- Reaction/corrective action plan required when process is not stable or capable
- Continuous improvement is required, particularly on special characteristics

*4.9.4 Modified Preliminary or Ongoing Capability Requirements
The Control Plan is to be annotated if the customer requires higher or lower capability requirements.

*4.9.5 Verification of Job Set-Ups
- Job set-ups are required to show that all produced parts meet requirements.
  - Documentation for set-up personnel
  - "Last-off" part comparison recommended
- Some customers may require statistical verification.

*4.9.6 Process Changes
- Changes to the process generally require prior customer approval. Refer to *Production Part Approval Process* Reference Manual, and to unique customer requirements.
- Maintain records of "change effective" dates.

*4.9.7 Appearance Items
You are to provide:
- Adequate/suitable lighting in inspection areas
- Master standards for appearance items, as needed

Continued on next page

- Adequate care of physical standards and equipment (4.11)
- Qualified personnel

Pitfalls

What is a Special Process?

A "special process" is one in which the product cannot be completely verified by later testing and inspection.

Additional attention to such processes, to ensure continued capability to meet specification, may include:

- Pre-qualification of the process and equipment
  - Identify all factors that affect the process, (including materials, operation, environment, utilities, machine controls), so that all potential variability affecting product quality can be controlled.
- Use of qualified personnel who meet specific training criteria
- Continuous monitoring and control of critical process characteristics
- Maintaining and analyzing records of processes, equipment, and personnel

4.10 Inspection and Testing

Why do it?

To make certain that product conforms to all requirements at each production stage; to identify nonconforming product at the earliest possible stage; and to facilitate corrective action.

What is it?

Demonstrating that inspection and test procedures are in operation to ensure that product conforms to specified requirements for:

- Incoming product
  - Procedures for inspection and verification
  - Holding or controlling until verified
  - The amount that you do depends upon the level of subcontractor control
- In-process product
  - Procedures for identifying and inspecting product
  - Process monitoring
  - Positive control until tests are complete
- Finished product
  - Procedures to ensure that all inspections and tests are completed
  - Product conforms to requirements
  - Product is not released until tests are completed

How do I do it?

1. Establish a separate plan or procedure for the following:
   • Receiving inspection and testing (consider the existing level of subcontractor control)
   • In-process inspection and testing
   • Final inspection and testing

2. Determine the policy, e.g., "Do not use until verified."

3. Identify categories of the product that are affected.

4. List all quality characteristics that are subject to inspection and test.

5. Ensure that the procedures for identifying specified requirements are available.

6. Provide for complete and current procedures at the point of inspection/test.

7. Provide for positive product identification/recall for urgent release.

8. Release product only when successful tests/records are complete.

9. Revise/improve procedures.

10. Evaluate revision.

Controlled Documents Needed
- Procedures for test and inspection criteria for:
  - Receiving inspection and testing
  - In-process inspection and testing
  - Final inspection and testing

Quality Records Needed
- Test results of inspection and testing
  - Incoming
  - In-process
  - Final
- Responsible authority for release noted

What else do I need to meet QS-9000?

*4.10.1 Acceptance Criteria
- Zero defects for attribute sampling plans; other situations require customer approval
- Accredited laboratories to be used if required by customer

*4.10.2 Incoming Product Quality
Requires one or more of the following:
- Statistical data
- Receiving inspection and/or testing
- Assessment of subcontractor by second or third party
- Part evaluation
- Warranty or certifications (If in conjunction with one of the above.)

QS-9000 Quality System Requirement

*4.10.4 Layout Inspection and Functional Testing
Requirements are established by the customer.

Pitfalls

- There is a lack of control at receiving, e.g., material that requires testing/inspection goes directly to inventory.
- Material that is released to production is not identified nor under complete control.
- Specified inspections or tests are not carried out.
- Records of inspection or test are missing.
- Final inspection or test is bypassed, or company product release procedures are bypassed.
- Reworked product is not fully reinspected.

4.11 Control of Inspection, Measuring, and Test Equipment

4.11.1 General
4.11.2 Control Procedure
*4.11.3 Inspection, Measuring, and Test
Equipment Records
*4.11.4 Measurement System Analysis
*QS-9000 Requirements

Why do it?

To make certain that inspection, measuring and test equipment is capable of consistently providing specified measurement requirements, so that proper decisions can be made for control and acceptance of product.

What is it?

Documented procedures to ensure that equipment is properly calibrated and will remain so. Also, it is the assurance that measurement uncertainty is known and consistent with required measurement capability.

How do I do it?

Refer to ISO 10012, "Quality Assurance Requirements for Measuring Equipment." See Chapter 5, page 159, for references.

1. **Identify all inspection and test requirements (4.10).**
   • Measurements to be made
   • Accuracy requirements

2. **List equipment and software available to conduct inspections/tests (fixed and portable).**
   • Laboratory equipment
   • Inspection and test equipment
   • Production machinery
   • Jigs, fixtures, templates
   • Test software

---

3. **Identify recognized calibration requirements and verification procedures for each piece of equipment**
   - Both fixed and portable equipment
   - Required measurement capability
   - Known measurement uncertainty
   - Calibration schedules

4. **Review and flowchart existing procedures and documentation for:**
   - Measurements to be made
   - Calibration procedures
   - "Measurement uncertainty"
   - Identification of calibration status on equipment
   - Out-of-calibration action
   - Work environment control
   - Handling and storage
   - Safeguarding against unauthorized adjustment
   - Rechecking intervals

5. **Revise/improve procedures.**

6. **Consider hard copy versus electronic records.**

7. **Establish an effective record system.**

8. **Evaluate revisions.**

Controlled Documents Needed
   - Required measurements and their accuracy
   - Listing of all measurement, inspection and test equipment affecting quality
   - Basis for calibration (National Standard)
   - Calibration process
   - Software verification process
   - Corrective action procedure
   - Verification and calibration schedule

Quality Records Needed

• Calibration and verification results

*4.11.3 Inspection, Measuring, and Test Equipment Records

• Revisions following engineering changes
• Gauge conditions and readings as received
• Customer notification of suspect material

*4.11.4 Measurement System Analysis

Statistical analysis of variability of equipment, e.g., gauge repeatability and reproducibility, is required. See the *Measurement Systems Analysis* Reference Manual, noted on page 157.

Pitfalls

• There is no real control system.
• No one is responsible for operating the system.
• Equipment that should be in the system is not in the system (particularly in research and development areas).
• Equipment is not identified.
• There is no traceability to a national or international standard.
• Not ensuring that adjustable equipment is not altered to invalidate calibration.
• When equipment is found out of calibration, no assessment is made on the impact on previous results.

4.12 Inspection and Test Status

* Product Location
* Supplemental Verification
    *QS-9000 Requirements

Why do it?

To make certain that only product that passes the required inspections and tests is released.

What is it?

Procedures for identifying inspection and test status, through production, installation, and servicing such as:

- Labels, tags, or stamps on product or labels
- Status cards
- Inspection records
- Software programs
- Product location

How do I do it?

1. **Identify locations where inspection status is critical, such as:**
   - Receiving
   - Production
   - Post production
   - Installation
   - Servicing

2. **Flowchart all processes.**
   See Flowcharting a Process, page 27.

3. **Determine the means of identification/status:**
   - Marking, stamps
   - Tags, labels
   - Routing cards

- Hard copy versus electronic records
- Physical location

4. **Review positive release procedures and responsibility.**

5. **Revise/improve the quality plan or procedures.**

6. **Evaluate revisions.**

Controlled Documents Needed
- Responsibilities for review and release
- Procedures for status process

Quality Records Needed
- Inspection results
- Releasing authority for conforming product

What else do I need to meet QS-9000?

Note: *The Control Plan may be your quality plan.*

*Product Location
The physical location of the product in the production process is not sufficient to indicate inspection status, unless it is clearly obvious, such as with an automatic process.

*Supplemental Verification
Your customer may set additional requirements.
                    QS-9000 Quality System Requirement

 Pitfalls

- Your control system is inadequate.
- You do not comply with your system, e.g., you have incomplete route cards.

4.13 Control of Nonconforming Product

Why do it?

To make certain that you do not use or unintentionally install nonconforming product.

What is it?

Procedures in operation that will help you:

- Identify nonconforming product.
- Evaluate degree and extent of the nonconformance.
- Segregate product physically, where practical, or through clear identification.
- Define who is responsible for authorizing disposition.
- Dispose of nonconforming product according to the quality plan or procedures. Dispose through:
  - Rework to meet specification
  - Repair to make fit for use but not as designed
  - Acceptance for use, with or without repair
  - Regrade for another application
  - Reject or scrap
- Notify concerned parties.

How do I do it?

1. **Review and document your procedures for the following:**
   - Identification
   - Documentation

- Segregation
- Prevention of inadvertent use/installation

2. **Document the procedures for disposition, notification, and classification.**

3. **Assign authority for disposition approval.**

4. **Document the procedures for reinspection of repairs or rework.**

5. **Document the concession reporting and handling procedures.**

6. **Revise and approve your procedures.**

7. **Evaluate revisions.**

Controlled Documents Needed
- Statement of responsibility for review and authority for disposition of nonconforming product
- Procedure for control of nonconforming product
- Statement in contract on authority for acceptance by waiver concession or repair

Quality Records Needed
- Results of investigation and disposition of nonconformance
- Reinspection of reworked or repaired product
- Notification of concerned parties
- Agreements of acceptance of waiver concessions

*Suspect Product
- Clause applies to suspect product as well as nonconforming product
- "Control Plan" may replace the quality plan

*4.13.3 Control of Reworked Product
- Rework instructions shall be available to, and in use by, appropriate personnel.
- A plan for reducing the amount of nonconforming product is to be in operation and progress tracked.
- Product supplied for service applications are to have no visible evidence of repair without approval.

Rework produces an item which is in every way indistinguishable from a "first-time-through" acceptable one.

Repair makes the item meet requirements but is different in some way, e.g., welded, from the original design.

*4.13.4 Engineering Approved Product Authorization
Changes in product or progress require customer approval, and apply also to subcontractor purchases. Specific product identification and records are to be kept, including the time interval during which the change is authorized.

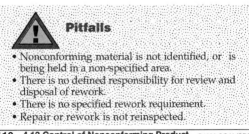

⚠ Pitfalls
- Nonconforming material is not identified, or is being held in a non-specified area.
- There is no defined responsibility for review and disposal of rework.
- There is no specified rework requirement.
- Repair or rework is not reinspected.

4.14 Corrective and Preventive Action

4.14.1 General
   * **Problem-Solving Methods**
4.14.2 Corrective Action
   * **Returned Product Test/Analysis**
4.14.3 Preventive Action
                          ***QS-9000 Requirements**

Why do it?

To make certain that causes of nonconforming product are investigated and an effort is made to eliminate them. You are also to attempt to detect and eliminate potential causes of nonconforming product before they occur. These actions contribute to continuous quality improvement.

What is it?

Investigation and elimination of causes of nonconforming product, at any point in the process, distribution, and installation. Also, it is the procedures in use to prevent *occurrence* of nonconforming product in the first place.

How do I do it?

1. **Separately identify procedures for corrective action (actual nonconformities) versus preventive action (potential nonconformities).**
   • Corrective action: go to step 2
   • Preventive action: go to step 3

2. **Carry out corrective action (see Problem-Solving/ Process- Improvement Model, page 26).**
   • Assign responsibility to an individual or team.
   • Review the number and significance of complaints and returns. Evaluate their importance.
   • Prepare a flowchart of the present system. (See Flowcharting a Process, page 27.)

- Evaluate the effectiveness of present practice.
- Provide resources:
  - Expertise
  - Records, instruction procedures
  - Defective product (for analysis)
- Revise/improve procedures to:
  - Investigate the cause of nonconformities
  - Analyze all processes
  - Determine a final "fix" (i.e., an action plan)
  - Initiate action to prevent recurrence
  - Apply new controls
- Make permanent changes.
- Evaluate revised procedures.

3. **Carry out preventive action. (See Problem-Solving/ Process- Improvement Model, page 26.)**
  ✓ • Assign responsibility to an individual or team.
  - Review existing preventive action activities.
  - Prepare a flowchart of the present system.
  - Evaluate the effectiveness of present practice.
  - Identify appropriate sources of information:
    - Reports of purchased materials' quality
    - Processes
    - Waiver concessions
    - Audit results
    - Quality records
    - Service reports
    - Customer complaints
  - Identify activities in which preventive action activities can be established or enhanced. Examples:
    - Product design
    - Process development
    - Process control
  - Make use of preventive action tools such as Failure Mode and Effects Analysis (FMEA).

- Modify and improve procedures to:
  - Identify potential nonconformities
  - Initiate action to prevent occurrence
  - Apply new controls
- Report preventive actions that are taken.
- Evaluate revised procedures.
- Follow up on the effectiveness of the actions taken.
- Submit actions for management review.

Controlled Documents Needed

✓ • Customer complaint handling procedures
✓ • Corrective action procedures
✓ • Preventive action procedures

Quality Records Needed

✓ • Record of nonconformances meriting assignment to the corrective action process
✓ • Customer complaints
✓ • Record of action taken on customer complaints
✓ • Corrective action investigation results
✓ • Record of preventive action meetings and results

What else do I need to meet QS-9000?

*Problem-Solving Methods
For product which has been identified as nonconforming by the customer, the supplier is to follow the problem-solving methods prescribed by the customer. (For a general problem-solving method, see page 26).

*Returned Product Test/Analysis
Parts that are returned from the customer are to be analyzed, with records kept, and appropriate corrective action and process change taken.

Pitfalls

- A corrective action plan exists on paper, but is not being followed.
- No person has been assigned responsibility for corrective/preventive action.
- No formal preventive action plan exists, especially one that addresses product and process development in particular.
- There is an emphasis on "troubleshooting" rather than prevention.
- The capability to prevent recurrence of product failures is inadequate.

Preventive and Corrective Action Problem-Solving Model

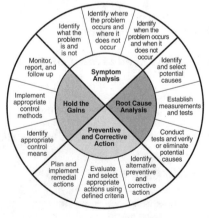

Information provided courtesy of Ross Gilbert, Kohler Company

4.15 Handling, Storage, Packaging, Preservation, and Delivery

Why do it?

To make certain that your procedures for handling, storage, packaging, preservation, and delivery of product are adequate, and to protect the integrity of product at all stages.

What is it?

Documented procedures at all stages, such as:

- Incoming materials
- In-process product
- Finished product
- Conditions during delivery as specified by the customer
- Prevention of damage or deterioration
- Secure storage and appropriate receipt and dispatch methods
- Packaging, packing, and marking processes
- Methods for preserving and segregating products
- Protection of product after inspection and test during storage and during delivery to destination

---

How do I do it?

1. Identify the critical points in the process.

2. Review available information, e.g., damage rates, shelf life.

3. Generate documentation for the following:
   - Packaging designs
   - Unique customer packaging requirements
   - In-process handling procedures
   - Packaging, packing, and marking processes
   - Warehouse procedures
   - Inventory/stock management procedures
   - Transportation techniques/carrier selection
   - Storage, preservation, and segregation methods
   - Environmental impact

4. Revise and improve procedures.

5. Evaluate revisions.

Controlled Documents Needed
   - Handling procedures
   - Storage procedures, including receipt and dispatch authorizations
   - Preservation requirements
   - Packaging requirements
   - Packaging, labels, and shipping container formats
   - Delivery requirements

Quality Records Needed
   - Verification of storage condition
   - Storage dates and expiration dates
   - Delivery dates as needed
   - Verification results on method of delivery

*4.15.3 Inventory

Inventory management system to optimize inventory turns and level and ensure stock rotation.

*4.15.4 Customer Packaging Standards

Packaging requirements established by customer.

*Labeling

Labeling requirements established by customer.

*4.15.6 Supplier Delivery Performance Monitoring

- Systems to support 100% on-time shipments. When not met, corrective action to improve delivery performance is necessary, with notification of customer.
- Lead times are to be established and met.
- Performance to delivery requirements to be tracked.
- Customer to specify the transportation mode, routing, and containers.

*Production Scheduling

Current orders are to drive production scheduling. Small lots (synchronous one-piece flow) are encouraged.

*Shipment Notification

On-line transmittal of advanced shipment notification required, with a backup method available.

Pitfalls

- Procedures are inadequate.
- Materials are: - Damaged/Corroded - Over-age - Unprotected - Unidentified - Nonconforming
- Lack of security, free access to a large inventory.
- Products damaged in delivery to customer.

Typical Elements of
Handling, Storage, Packaging,
Preservation, and Delivery

Handling	• Protect the product using containers, pallets, or work platforms. • Install and maintain conveyors and other automated transfer systems for product protection. • Train operators in awareness of product protection. • Operate lift trucks, loaders, and other vehicles in a safe manner to minimize damage.
Storage	• Provide adequate space and facilities. • Ensure cleanliness. • Maintain an appropriate environment (temperature, humidity). • Provide appropriate security and access to storage areas. • Provide for appropriate identification marking and traceability.
Packaging	• Develop unit pack and master packs to provide appropriate protection while in supplier's plant and during shipping. • Provide markings for identification and traceability, where appropriate.
Preservation	• Control the environment (temperature, humidity). • Segregate product where necessary.
Delivery	• Provide for proper protection after release, until supplier is no longer responsible for distribution handling, per contract. • Consider the delivery method. • Control the environment (temperature, humidity). • Provide security during delivery.

Adapted from Demystifying ISO 9000, Information Mapping's Guide to the ISO 9000 Standards, *p. 2-56*

4.16 Control of Quality Records

* Record Retention
* Superseded Parts

*QS-9000 Requirements

Why do it?

To make certain that your quality records demonstrate effective operation of your quality system, which will ensure the achievement of required product quality.

What is it?

Effective control of quality records through documented procedures. It includes:

- Storing your records effectively
- Establishing record retention times
- Making quality records available for evaluation by the customer, if required
- Ensuring that records are legible and easily retrievable

Records may be hard copy, electronic, or other media.

How do I do it?

1. Review the list of documents (4.5).

2. For each category (function) of documents, review procedures to:
   - Identify quality records
   - Collect quality records
   - Index quality records
   - Provide access to quality records
   - File quality records
   - Store quality records
   - Maintain quality records
   - Dispose of quality records

---

3. **Include a review of the following:**
   - Supplier records
   - Subcontractor records
   - Installation and servicing records

4. **For each document category, establish the following issues about the documents:**
   - Legibility
   - Identification with a product
   - Ability to be retained
   - Storage environment
   - Retention needs
   - Availability to the customer

5. **Review requirements for quality records under the following clauses:**
   4.1.3, 4.2, 4.3.4, 4.4, 4.6.2, 4.7, 4.8, 4.9, 4.10, 4.11, 4.12, 4.13, 4.14, 4.17, and 4.18

Controlled Documents Needed
   - Procedures for control of quality records
   - Index of records
   - Retention schedule for records

Quality Records Needed
   (All of the records from all the clauses.)
   - Record of management reviews
   - Record of disposition
   - Inspection reports
   - Test data
   - Qualification reports
   - Validation reports
   - Audit reports
   - Material review reports
   - Calibration data
   - Quality cost reports

What else do I need to meet QS-9000?

*Record Retention

- Production part approvals, tooling records, and purchase orders must be retained one calendar year after time requirements for production and service. These must include production part approvals, tooling records, and purchase orders.

- Quality performance records are to be retained one year beyond the year created.

- Internal quality system audits and management reviews are to be retained for three years.

- The above record retention requirements do not supersede customer or government regulations.

- Specified periods are "minimums."

*Superseded Parts

The "new part" file is to contain documents from superseded parts if they are required for a new part qualification.

QS-9000 Quality System Requirement

 **Pitfalls**

- No records exist.
- Records are not readily available.
- Records are not legible.
- No retention periods have been established.

Control of Quality Records

Identification	Designation of individual records.
Collection	Responsibility for record collection.
Indexing	An indexing structure providing an access trail.
Access	Provision for ready access of quality records for those using them.
Filing	Filing quality records where access is easy, during the high review part of the record's life.
Storage	Less accessible bulk storage during archival part of record life.
Maintenance	Records are to demonstrate conformance to specified requirements and effective quality system operation. Subcontractor quality records may be an element of such data.
Legibility	Readable under normal operating conditions.
Retention times	Established, recorded, and administered.
Form of records	Hard copy, electronic, or other media.

©1996 GOAL/QPC

4.17 Internal Quality Audits

* Inclusion of Working Environment
*QS-9000 Requirements

Why do it?

To make certain that your quality activities meet requirements and demonstrate the effectiveness of your quality system. This strives to ensure the continued capability of all elements of quality practice.

What is it?

A plan and procedures for conducting internal audits of your quality system.

- Schedule audits according to status and importance of activity.
- Carry out audits using independent personnel.
- Document audit results and any follow-up.
- Communicate audit results to appropriate personnel, including management.
- Initiate corrective action.
- Verify and record effectiveness of the corrective action taken.

How do I do it?

Refer to ISO 10011-1, 10011-2, and 10011-3, "Guidelines for Auditing Quality Systems." See Chapter 5, page 159.

1. Identify the activities to be audited.

2. Establish the qualifications of audit personnel, including:
   - Experience
   - Training
   - Availability
   - Independence

3. **Develop (or update) audit procedures to include:**
   - Planning
   - Documentation

4. **Conduct an initial (trial) quality audit.**
   - Evaluate the adequacy of procedures.
   - Determine the effectiveness of the procedures.
   - Verify compliance.
   - Determine the suitability of the working environment.

5. **Establish a permanent quality audit program.**

Controlled Documents Needed
   - Internal audit plan
   - Internal audit schedule
   - Procedures for conducting an internal audit
   - List of qualified auditors

Quality Records Needed
   - Audit reports
   - Record of management audit review
   - Record of corrective action taken

What else do I need to meet QS-9000?

*Inclusion of Working Environment
Internal audits will include working environment as an audit element.

Pitfalls

- No system exists.
- There is no corrective action on findings.
- Auditors used are not trained.
- No independent person is present to conduct the audit.
- Records are incomplete.

Establishing an Internal Quality Audit Process

- Develop an overall audit plan.
- Assign audit personnel.
- Schedule audits on the basis of importance and status.
- Review the effectiveness of any previous corrective action.
- Conduct the audit.
- Submit the audit report to management.
- Management to review noncompliances.
- Management to take corrective action on non-compliances.

"Checks and Balances" to Ensure Continued Effective Use of ISO 9001

After registration to ISO 9001, suppliers are to ensure that the requirements continue to be met. Three activities provide for this continuance:

- Internal Quality Audits (4.17)
- Periodic Management Review (4.1.3)
- Scheduled surveillance visits by the registrar

4.18 Training

* Training as a Strategic Issue
*QS-9000 Requirements

Why do it?

To make certain that employees are trained to do their jobs effectively, so they may avoid mistakes that affect quality.

What is it?

A training process in use that is based on your quality system job requirements. Elements include training needs, training of personnel to meet those needs, keeping records of individual qualifications, and development of a training plan.

How do I do it?

1. **Identify training needs:**
   - List all job functions
   - Establish training requirements for each function
   - Include the requirements in job descriptions

2. **Provide training based on:**
   - Quality plan elements
   - Process knowledge requirements: methods, equipment
   - Product knowledge requirements: specifications, workmanship standards
   - Cross-training
   - Extent of trainee's knowledge and skills
   - Other requirements: internal customer, delivery

3. **Establish and record personnel qualifications in individual personnel file to include:**
   - All required training completed
   - Education (initial, additional)
   - Previous experience
   - Physical characteristics and limitations
   - Special training (safety, SPC)

- Medical records
- Awards, rewards, promotions
- Cross-training

4. **Develop and document a training plan (matrix) to include:**
   - Required training
   - Optional additional training
   - Qualifications of trainers
   - Periodic evaluation of effectiveness

Controlled Documents Needed
- Quality system training needs
- Training procedures
- Training modules
- List of qualified trainers, by skill

Quality Records Needed
- Personnel qualifications
- Training plans for operators
- Required training certifications

What else do I need to meet QS-9000?

*Training as a Strategic Issue
- Since training affects everyone, it should be considered as a strategic issue.
- Evaluate training effectiveness.

 Pitfalls

- No records exist or records are inadequate.
- There is a lack of appropriate education, training, or experience.
- Training needs are not assessed.

Example of a Matrix for Quality Education and Training in Japan

Topic \ People	Top Management	Middle Mgmt/ Staff	Engineers	Supervisors	Function & Administration	General Workers
TQM Concepts	○	○	○	○	○ / ◎	○
TQM Techniques	○	○	◎	◎		○
Statistical Methods	○	○	◎	○	○	○
Quality Assurance	△	○	◎	○	△	△
Product Development	△	△	◎		△ / ○	
Role in TQM	◎	◎	◎	◎	◎	◎
QC Circle	△	○	△	◎	△	○ / ◎
New Product Introduction	○	△	◎	○		
Hoshin Planning	◎	○	△		△	
Company Production System			○	◎		○

Educated to: △ = Understand   ○ = Use   ◎ = Master

Excerpt from GOAL/QPC Research Committee Research Report, "Total Quality Control Education in Japan," p. 9

Partial Example of a Knowledge, Skills, and Abilities Matrix

Legend:
- (R) Required
- (D) Desirable
- (NA) Not Applicable
- (94) Year Scheduled
- (C) Completed

Dept #/name: 570 — Quality Systems

Category	Course	Hrs.	Director — Manos, K	Quality Manager — Vance, B	Quality Manager — Booker, B	Sr. Quality Engnr — McMurray, D	Sr. Quality Engnr — Smith, G
Quality	Process Activity Analysis	4 hrs.	na	na	D	C	C
Quality	Project Mgmt.	24 hrs.	na	95	D	C	C
Quality	GDT Overview (Managers course)	16 hrs.	na	na	D	D	C
Quality	GDT Specifier	40 hrs.	na	na	D	D	C
Quality	GDT Interpreter	24 hrs.	na	na	D	na	C
Quality	Reliability in Prod. Design/Test	24 hrs.	na	na	R	R	95
Quality	QFD	2 hrs.	na	na	R	R	C
Quality	FMEA	4 hrs.	na	96	R	94	C
Quality	DOE	32 hrs.	na	na	R	94	95
Quality	Chart Interpretation	4 hrs.	na	na	R	C	C
Quality	Pre-Control	2 hrs.	na	na	R	C	C
Quality	Basic SPC Charting	10 hrs.	na	na	R	C	C
Quality	Process Capability /Dist. Analysis	24 hrs.	na	na	R	C	C
Quality	Mfg. Planning Process Control	2 hrs.	na	na	R	C	C
Members Who Supervise/Manage Others	Managing Personal Growth (D)	13 hrs.	R	94	R	D	C
Members Who Supervise/Manage Others	Managing Diversity (D)	9 hrs.	R	94	94	95	C
Members Who Supervise/Manage Others	Selection Interviewing (D)	12 hrs.	R	94	95	96	C
Members Who Supervise/Manage Others	Quality Improvement Fac. (D)	4 hrs.	R	95	94	na	C
Members Who Supervise/Manage Others	Performance Appraisal Trng. (R)	6 hrs.	R	95	C	95	C
Members Who Supervise/Manage Others	Haworth Policies (R)	4 hrs.	R	95	C	95	C
Members Who Supervise/Manage Others	Delegation (R)	8 hrs.	R	94	C	95	C
Members Who Supervise/Manage Others	Conflict Resolution (R)	16 hrs.	R	94	94	94	C
Members Who Supervise/Manage Others	Managing Change (R)	16 hrs.	R	94	94	94	C
Members Who Supervise/Manage Others	Interpersonal Mgmt. Skills (R)	12 hrs.	R	94	C	97	C
Members Who Supervise/Manage Others	Sexual Harassment (R)	4 hrs.	R	94	C	95	C
Members Who Supervise/Manage Others	Affirmative Action/EEO (R)	4 hrs.	R	94	C	95	C
All Members	Sexual Harrassment (nonmgmt) (D)	4 hrs.	R	na	R	C	na
All Members	JIT (R)	12 hrs.	R	94	R	C	C
All Members	IDEAS Suggestion System (R)	2 hrs.	R	94	R	C	C
All Members	4-Step Problem Solving (R)	12 hrs.	R	C	R	C	C
All Members	Hazard Comm/Right to Know (R)	1 hr.	R	C	R	C	C
All Members	Recall Orientation (R)	7.5 hrs.	R	94	R	C	C
All Members	First Day Orientation (R)	6.5 hrs.	R	C	R	C	C

Information provided courtesy of William J. Vance, Haworth, Inc., Holland, MI

4.19 Servicing

* Feedback of Information from Service
*QS-9000 Requirements

Why do it?

To make certain that after-sale attention is provided for your product, when required, to ensure complete customer satisfaction.

What is it?

Documented procedures for servicing, to verify that servicing meets specified requirements.

- Because you need to treat servicing as an extension of your quality system, many or all of the sections of the standard may apply.

How do I do it?

1. Identify customer service requirements.

2. Document the service requirements:
   - Establish procedures
   - Perform the service
   - Report and verify that the requirements are met

3. Revise and improve procedures.

4. Evaluate revisions.

Controlled Documents Needed

- Servicing requirements
- Servicing procedures and manuals
- Service personnel training requirements
- Measurement equipment and calibration procedures

Quality Records Needed

- Personnel training results and certifications
- Measurement equipment and calibration results
- Corrective action
- Service records

What else do I need to meet QS-9000?

*Feedback of Information from Service

Information from service should be communicated to manufacturing, engineering, and design.

Pitfalls

- There is a lack of liaison between the service department and the main company.
- There are no procedures.
- Procedures are incomplete.
- Field measurement equipment is inadequate compared to equipment used in the factory.

Typical Elements of Servicing

- Control of service manuals
- Training and certification of personnel
- Supply of service parts
- Calibration of test equipment
- Corrective action
- Quality auditing of activities
- Management review of audit findings
- Service records

4.20 Statistical Techniques

4.20.1 Identification of Need
4.20.2 Procedures
* **Selection of Statistical Tools**
* **Knowledge of Basic Statistical Concepts**

*QS-9000 Requirement

Why do it?

To make certain that you have identified places in you
process where the use of statistical techniques are necessar
to ensure quality or to detect potential problems.

What is it?

A process for identifying the need for statistical technique
that are required for establishing, controlling, an
verifying process capability and product quality. Wher
the need is established, you are to maintain and documer
procedures for these statistical techniques, to ensure tha
they are correctly applied.

How do I do it?

1. Identify existing statistical applications an
   procedures.

2. Review status, correctness, and effectiveness c
   statistical technique applications such as in:
   • Establishing process capability
   • Identifying potential problems
   • Verifying product characteristics

3. Examine the quality plan for additional application

4. Provide for additional statistical applications.

5. Establish a training plan.

6. Select training personnel.

'. Conduct training sessions.

3. Evaluate the effectiveness and value of new applications.

Controlled Documents Needed

- Process for determining a need for statistical techniques
- Listing of applications of statistical techniques

Quality Records Needed

- Results of statistical techniques that are applied

What else do I need to meet QS-9000?

*4.20.2 Selection of Statistical Tools
Statistical tools to be used are to be identified during quality planning, and to be included in the Control Plan.

*Knowledge of Basic Statistical Concepts
- As appropriate, concepts such as variability, control, capability, and over-adjustment should be understood.
- Consult the *Fundamental Statistical Process Control* Reference Manual (Chapter 5, page 157).

QS-9000 Quality System Requirement

 Pitfalls

- Not using statistical techniques when they are necessary.
- Ineffective use of statistical methods.
- Ineffective use of sampling systems.

Typical Applications of Statistical Methods

Guidance from ISO 9004-1

- Market analysis
- Product design
- Dependability specification, longevity, and durability prediction
- Process-control and process-capability studies
- Determination of quality levels in sampling plans
- Data analysis, performance assessment, and nonconformity analysis
- Process improvement
- Safety evaluation and risk analysis
- Trend identification
- Cause-effect relationship identification

Typical Statistical Techniques Useful in Operations

Guidance from ISO 9000-2 and ISO 9004-1

- Design of experiments and factorial analysis, to identify variables
- Analysis of variance and regression analysis, to provide quantitative process models
- Tests of significance, for decision making
- Quality control charts and CUSUM techniques, for monitoring, control, and measurement
- Statistical sampling, for acceptance and cost control
- Graphical methods, for diagnosis

Tools and Techniques for Quality Improvement

Consult the listing of resources on the next page to match up a letter (A,B,C, etc.) with the name of the resource.

Tool	Reference*				Resources
Statistical Tools	ISO 9004-1	QS-9000	ISO 9000-2	ISO 9004-4	
Analysis of variance (ANOVA)	•		•		D, E, F, G, M
Control charts - attributes	•	•	•	•	C, E, F, H, I, L, N
Control charts - variables	•	•	•	•	C, E, F, H, I, L, N
Capability indices (C_p, C_{pk})		•			C, E, H, L, N
Cumulative sum chart (CUSUM)	•	•			E, F, G
Design of experiments (DOE)	•	•	•		D, F, G, O
Evolutionary operation of processes (EVOP)		•			F, P
Histogram		•			C, F, H, L, N
Pareto diagram			•	•	C, F, L, N
Regression analysis	•		•		D, F, G, O
Scatter diagram			•	•	C, F, H, L
Statistical sampling	•				E, F, G, H
Tests of significance	•				D, F, G, O
Non-Statistical Tools	ISO 9004-1	QS-9000	ISO 9000-2	ISO 9004-4	
Affinity diagram				•	C, K, L
Benchmarking		•		•	A, B
Brainstorming				•	C, L
Cause and effect diagram (Ishikawa)				•	C, H, L, N
Flowchart				•	C, L, N
FMEA		•			See manuals on p. 157
Problem solving		•			C, L
Theory of constraints		•			J
Tree diagram				•	C, K, L

*See the list of standards in Chapter 5, page 159

The black circle [•] indicates that the document makes a reference to the use of the tool.

Tools & Techniques Resource List

See the matrix on the previous page to locate a specific tool o technique, the ISO or QS-9000 document it is referenced in, and i which resource book(s) you may find the tool described (indicate by letters A, B, C, etc.).

A. *Benchmarking: The Search for Industry Best Practices that Lead* *Superior Performance*, Robert Camp, Quality Press, Milwauke WI, 1989.

B. *Benchmarking*, GOAL/QPC Research Committee Report, Methuen, MA, 1991.

C. *Coach's Guide to The Memory Jogger™ II: The Easy-to-Use, Comple Reference for Working with Improvement and Planning Tools Teams*, Michael Brassard, Diane Ritter, and others, GOAL QPC, Methuen, MA, 1995.

D. *Fundamental Concepts in the Design of Experiments*, Charle Hicks, Holt, Reinhart and Winston, New York, 1982.

E. *Fundamental Statistical Process Control* Reference Manual, For Chrysler, General Motors, Southfield, MI, 1992.

F. *Juran's Quality Control Handbook*, 4th ed., J. M. Juran & Fran Gryna, eds., McGraw-Hill Publishing Co., New York, 198

G. *Quality Control and Industrial Statistics*, Acheson J. Dunca Irwin Professional Publishing, Homewood, IL, 1986.

H. *SPC Simplified: Practical Steps to Quality*, Davida M. Amsde Robert T. Amsden, & Howard E. Butler, Quality Resource White Plains, NY, 1989.

I. *Statistical Quality Control*, 7th ed., Eugene L. Grant & Richard Leavenworth, McGraw-Hill Publishing Co., New York, 199

J. *The Goal: A Process of Ongoing Improvement*, Eliyahu M. Goldratt Jeff Cox, North River Press, Inc., Croton-on-Hudson, NY, 199

K. *The Memory Jogger Plus+®*, Michael Brassard, GOAL/QP(Methuen, MA, 1989.

L. *The Memory Jogger™ II*, Michael Brassard & Diane Ritter, GOAL QPC, Methuen, MA, 1994.

M. *Understanding Industrial Experimentation*, Donald Wheeler, SP Press, Knoxville, TN, 1988.

N. *Understanding Statistical Process Control*, 2nd ed., David Chambe & Donald Wheeler, SPC Press, Knoxville, TN, 1992.

O. *Handbook of Statistical Method for Engineers and Scientist* Harrison Wadsworth, ed., McGraw-Hill Publishing Co., Ne York, 1990.

P. *Evolutionary Operation: A Statistical Method for Proces Improvement*, George Box and Norman Draper, John Wiley Sons, New York, 1969.

Production Part Approval Process
- *Production Part Approval Process* Reference Manual is a requirement of QS-9000.
- Changes from the original approval require notification and possible resubmittal.
- Suppliers are responsible for subcontractor materials and services.
- "Appearance Items" requires separate approval.
- Engineering changes are to be validated.

Continuous Improvement
- Philosophy of continuous improvement is to include timing, delivery, price, and impact on all business and support activities.
- An action plan is required.
- For attribute characteristics, continuous improvement means perfection of process methods.
- For variables, continuous improvement means meeting target values and reducing variation.

Opportunities for improvement
- Machine downtime
- Machine changeover times
- Excessive cycle time
- Scrap, rework, and repair
- Use of floor space
- Excessive variation
- Less than 100% first-run capability
- Process averages not centered on target values
- Testing requirements not justified
- Labor and materials waste
- Excessive non-quality cost
- Difficult assembly or installation

- Excessive handling and storage
- new target values
- measurement system capability
- customer dissatisfaction

Techniques for continuous improvement

Supplier to demonstrate knowledge of, and use when appropriate:

- Capability indices (C_p, C_{pk})
- Control charts (variables, attributes)
- Cumulative sum charting (CUSUM)
- Design of experiments (DOE)
- Evolutionary operation of processes (EVOP)
- Theory of constraints
- Overall equipment effectiveness
- Cost of quality
- Parts per million (PPM) analysis
- Value analysis
- Problem solving
- Benchmarking
- Analysis of motion/ergonomics
- Mistake proofing

Descriptions of these techniques may be found in *The Memory Jogger™ II*, or the automotive Big Three reference manuals (see p. 157), or other statistical and quality text

3. Manufacturing Capabilities

Facilities, equipment, and process planning, and their effectiveness

A cross-functional team approach is to consider:

- Plant layout
- Overall work plan
- Automation
- Ergonomics

- Line balance
- Production inventory levels
- Labor content

Mistake proofing

- Processes, product, facilities, equipment and tooling needs are to be addressed at the planning stage.

Tool design and fabrication
Require appropriate resources for:

- Design
- Fabrication
- Dimensional inspection
- Tracking and follow-up of subcontractors
- Identification of customer-owned tools and equipment

Tool management
The control system is to include:

- Maintenance and repair facilities and personnel
- Storage and recovery
- Set-up
- Tool change programs for perishable tools

Note: *At intervals, the International Automotive Sector Group publishes "sanctioned QS-9000 interpretations" that are binding to those required to use QS-9000.*

QS-9000 Reference Manual Matrix

QS-9000 refers to five automotive Big Three reference manuals* (see p. 157) and also requires use of a Control Plan. This matrix provides a guideline to ISO 9001 and QS-9000 clauses where their use may be helpful.

Statistical Process Control (SPC)*	Measurement Systems Analysis (MSA)*	Failure Mode Effects Analysis (FMEA)*	Control Plan (CP)	Advanced Product Q Planning (APQP)*	Production Part Approval Process (PPAP)*		
			X	X	X	4.1	Management Responsibility
X		X	X	X	X	4.2	Quality System
X					X	4.3	Contract Review
X	X	X	X	X	X	4.4	Design Control
X					X	4.5	Document and Data Control
X					X	4.6	Purchasing
X			X		X	4.7	Control of Customer-Supplied Product
X			X			4.8	Product Identification and Traceability
X	X	X	X	X	X	4.9	Process Control
X			X		X	4.10	Inspection and Testing
X	X	X	X		X	4.11	Control of Inspection and Testing Equipment
			X		X	4.12	Inspection and Test Status
X			X		X	4.13	Control of Nonconforming Product
X			X		X	4.14	Corrective and Preventive Action
X			X		X	4.15	Handling, Storage, Packaging, Preservation, and Delivery
X			X		X	4.16	Control of Quality Records
X			X			4.17	Internal Quality Audits
			X		X	4.18	Training
X			X		X	4.19	Servicing
X			X		X	4.20	Statistical Techniques

Information provided courtesy of Robert Belfit, Jr., Omni Tech International, Ltd., Midland, MI

Chapter 4

ISO 9000 and Continuous Improvement Efforts

Continuing to Improve After ISO 9000 Registration

ISO 9000 requires that you have in place a quality system that assures your customers that your organization has the *capability* of providing quality products and/or services. The standards, basically, require that you document your processes and then follow them as stated. The standards *do not*, however, ensure that the products and/or services produced from your processes are quality ones.

The standards, however, do form a necessary *foundation* for achieving quality products and services that will satisfy customers. The standards are key to:

- Documenting your processes
- Establishing controls of the processes
- Providing discipline to adhere to your processes

Securing ISO 9000 registration should be considered a milestone toward a comprehensive quality management system. Soon after completing adoption of ISO 9001 or ISO 9002, your organization should consider the various options for improvement. They include using:

- ISO 9001 for continuing improvement
- ISO 9004-1, Quality Management and Quality System Elements – Guidelines
- ISO 9004-4 (10004) Guidelines for Quality Improvement
- QS-9000, Quality System Requirements
- Malcolm Baldrige National Quality Award criteria
- Other quality approaches

The first step is to survey your organization's existing capabilities, using one or more of these approaches. Then, just as with the original planning for ISO 9001 registration, a plan for adopting a continuous improvement system should be developed and followed.

Using ISO 9001 for Continuous Quality Improvement

The ISO 9001 standard has implied requirements for continuous improvement built into it. The frequently used phrase *"Say what you do, do what you say"* is often used to describe ISO 9001. The phrase falls short of the intent of the 1994 edition of the standard, however, because the phrase implies that it is necessary only to adhere to established procedures.

The ISO 9001 standard contains elements that are linked in a cycle of continuous improvement:

Objectives for Quality (4.1.1)

Management Review (4.1.3)

Internal Audits (4.17)

Corrective and Preventive Action (4.14)

Five themes are also contained in ISO 9001:

- Objectives for quality, and ensuring the effectiveness of the quality system
- Continual improvement
- Balance between documentation, skills, and training
- Design control
- Statistical techniques

To use ISO 9001 effectively as a continual improvement tool, follow the Plan-Do-Check-Act cycle (see page 15).

- **PLAN** your objectives for quality, and the processes to achieve them.
- **DO** the appropriate resource allocation, implementation, training, and documentation.

Continued on next page

- **CHECK** to see if:
  - You are implementing as planned
  - Your quality system is effective
  - You are meeting your objectives for quality
- **ACT** to improve the system as needed.

Thus, ISO 9001 is seen as a tool for growth and improvement in capability. You should make use of the tools you might already have in place. These include:

Setting objectives for quality. These include both product and system improvements related to operating efficiencies and ultimately to cost control (see "4.1 Management Responsibility," page 50).

Internal Quality Audit. Perform periodic auditing to verify that all systems are in place and continue to be effective, and so opportunities for systems improvements can be noted and action taken (see "4.17 Internal Quality Audits," page 123).

Management Review. Provide for annual review of program status, including the effectiveness of internal auditing. This is a time for goal setting (see "4.1 Management Responsibility," page 50).

Corrective Action. Identify nonconformances, both internal and external, as signals of opportunities for improvement, making process and product changes to prevent recurrence (see "4.14.2 Corrective Action," page 111).

Preventive Action. Identify potential problems before they occur by identifying deviations in patterns or trends in product or process performance. These trends may point to opportunities for improvement in product or process design. (see "4.14.3 Preventive Action," page 112).

Information adapted from a paper by Donald Marquardt, Marquardt and Associates, Wilmington, DE

Use of ISO 9004-1 as a Tool for Quality Improvement

The ISO 9004-1 standard, "Quality Management and Quality System Elements – Guidelines," is one of the original family of ISO 9000 standards; it was developed simultaneously with ISO 9001. The 9004-1 standard covers essentially all the elements in ISO 9001, and typically provides more comprehensive detail. In addition, ISO 9004-1 addresses subjects such as financial considerations, quality in marketing, product safety, and a subclause on quality improvement. The "life cycle" approach of ISO 9004-1 is shown in the diagram below.

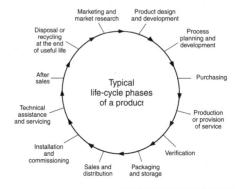

ANSI/ISO/ASQC Q 9004-1:1994, p. 5

ISO 9004-1 is practical to use as a next step in improving quality management capability for companies registered to ISO 9001. However, an alternative for the company that has not begun the ISO 9001 registration process is to build its quality system around ISO 9004-1, having it in full operation before addressing the registration needs of ISO 9001. ISO identifies this process in the publication titled "Implementing ISO 9000." Copies are available from the ANSI Publications Department (see Chapter 5, page 157).

Using QS-9000 as a Quality Improvement Tool

For decades, Chrysler, Ford, and General Motors hav[e] required their suppliers not only to meet produc[t] specifications but to follow prescribed quality system[s] and procedures.

These practices cover the spectrum from produc[t] development through statistical process contro[l] techniques, to effective response to customer feedback[.] These automobile companies have years of experience i[n] determining which quality systems their suppliers shoul[d] follow to provide assurance that they are capable o[f] delivering products that meet the companies' requirements[.]

With the advent of the ISO 9001 standard, these thre[e] companies, who had already been coordinating projects[,] made the decision to require their suppliers to meet ISO 9001.

In addition, there were certain other quality system requirements recognized as important to their uniqu[e] industry needs. These needs were incorporated wit[h] ISO-9001 to form the QS-9000. Also, reference manual[s] were prepared to give guidance to suppliers.

The types of additions to ISO 9001 contained in QS-900[0] Requirements include:

- *Interpretations:* explaining the "meaning" of ISO 9001 statements as they apply to the auto industry without changing basic requirements.

- *Prescriptive statements:* "how to," such as specifi[c] methods of process control, including control charts[.]

Certain sector-specific requirements that go beyond ISO 9001 content have also been identified. These are contained in Section II of QS-9000. These requirements are summarized on page 137.

Customer-specific requirements are contained in Section III of QS-9000. (See Chapter 5, "Additional Resources," page 157 for ordering the QS-9000 Requirements.) *The Memory Jogger™ 9000* does not summarize the customer-specific requirements, but suppliers to those companies will be required to meet them.

Because of the nature of the supplemental requirements in QS-9000, even those organizations that do not sell to the auto industry may be well advised to consider those elements as a basis for improving their quality capabilities. Certainly organizations should review these requirements, and determine which of them apply to their industry.

Note: *A separate standard on quality improvement has been published by ISO, designated ISO 9004-4 (10004) "Guidelines for Quality Improvement."*

Malcolm Baldrige National Quality Award

Each year since 1988, a set of criteria has been published as foundation for the examination process for America's Malcolm Baldrige National Quality Award (MBNQA) for which organizations may apply.

The most visible part of the award program is the process of evaluating and selecting outstanding organizations that meet the stringent criteria of the award. (The criteria for the 1996 MBNQA are listed on the next page.)

Awards are presented each year by the President of the United States. Winners publicly describe the actions they took to become outstanding in their field. Similar award programs are in use in Europe, many nations, and a large number of states.

Many organizations are using the criteria of the MBNQA to judge their own present capabilities (self-assessment) and in setting goals for improvements in quality. Criteria are updated each year, hence, they express state-of-the-art developments in quality management practice. The booklet describing the criteria is available at no cost from the National Institute of Standards and Technology office. Contact:

> Malcolm Baldrige National Quality Award
> National Institute of Standards and Technology
> Route 270 and Quince Orchard Road
> Administration Building, Room A537
> Gaithersburg, MD 20899-0001
> **Phone:** (301) 975-2036

Bulk quantities are available at low cost from ASQC. Case studies developed for examiner training, and videos describing winners, are also available. (See Chapter 5, "Additional Resources," page 156 for ASQC's address.)

1996 MBNQA Criteria

1.0 Leadership
1.1 Senior Executive Leadership
1.2 Leadership System and Organization
1.3 Public Responsibility and Corporate Citizenship

2.0 Information and Analysis
2.1 Management of Information and Data
2.2 Competitive Comparisons and Benchmarking
2.3 Analysis and Use of Company-Level Data

3.0 Strategic Planning
3.1 Strategy Development
3.2 Strategy Deployment

4.0 Human Resource Development and Management
4.1 Human Resource Planning and Evaluation
4.2 High Performance Work Systems
4.3 Employee Education, Training, and Development
4.4 Employee Well-Being and Satisfaction

5.0 Process Management
5.1 Design and Introduction of Products and Services
5.2 Process Management: Product and Service Production and Delivery
5.3 Process Management: Support Services
5.4 Management of Supplier Performance

6.0 Business Results
6.1 Product and Service Quality Results
6.2 Company Operational and Financial Results
6.3 Human Resource Results
6.4 Supplier Performance Results

7.0 Customer Focus and Satisfaction
7.1 Customer and Market Knowledge
7.2 Customer Relationship Management
7.3 Customer Satisfaction Determination
7.4 Customer Satisfaction Results

How Does ISO 9001 Align with MBNQA?

Legend: ○ Very well aligned · ◐ Somewhat aligned · ● Little/no alignment · ★ At odds

ISO 9001 Quality System Standard	1.1	1.2	1.3	2.1	2.2	2.3	3.1	3.2	4.1	4.2	4.3	4.4	5.1	5.2	5.3	5.4	6.1	6.2	6.3	6.4	7.1	7.2	7.3	7.4
	Leadership			Information and Analysis			Strategic Planning		Human Resource Development and Management				Process Management				Business Results				Customer Focus and Satisfaction			
4.1 Mgt. Resp.	●	●		○	●	●	○	●	●	●			●	●	●		●	●	●	●	○	○	○	○
4.2 Q System		○		○	●	●	○		●	●	●		●	●	●	○		○	○	●	○	○		
4.3 Contract Rev.						○	○						●	●	○	○				○	●	○		
4.4 Design						○							●	●					○	○	●			
4.5 Docmnt/Data						○							○			○				○				
4.6 Purchasing					○	○								○		○			○	●				
4.7 Cust. Product						○							●							○				
4.8 Product ID						○							●	●		○				○				
4.9 Process						○					○		●	●	●	○			●	○				
4.10 Insp/Test					○	○							○		●	○				○				
4.11 Insp. Eqpmt.					○	○							●			○				○				
4.12 Insp. Status					○	○							○	●		○				○				○
4.13 Noncorf. Prod.						○							○	●		●								
4.14 Corr. Prev.	●					○	○			○		○	○	○	●	●	●	●	○	○	●	●	●	●
4.15 Handling					○								○			○								
4.16 Q Records		○			○	○	○						●	●		●	○	○		○				
4.17 Q Audits		●	●		○	○	●	●									○			○				●
4.18 Training		●	●			○								○	○									
4.19 Servicing						○					○	○	●	●	●	○			●	●		●	●	●
4.20 Statistics	○	○		○	●	●	○		○	○	○	○	○	○	○	●	○	○	○		○	○	●	●

Adapted from the ISO 9000 Handbook, Irwin Professional Publishing, 1994, pp. 334-5 (Updated to the 1996 MBNQA criteria)

ISO 9000 Standards and MBNQA

- ISO 9000 is more specific in the procedural items that are covered.

- The ISO 9000 standards make some reference to most categories in the Baldrige Award criteria, including leadership, quality planning, human resource utilization, and quality satisfaction.

- The ISO 9000 standards do not have specific references to quality results and measuring customer satisfaction.

- The 1994 ISO 9000 standards now make reference to continuous quality improvement, where previously, they did not.

- ISO 9000 sets a standard that most of the better organizations of the world can be expected to follow in practice.

- The Baldrige Award criteria represent world-class performance.

Other Quality Approaches

Many organizations choose to adopt a philosophical approach to achieving quality improvement. Following the teachings of one or more of the quality gurus (Dr. W. Edwards Deming, Dr. Joseph M. Juran, Philip B. Crosby, Dr. Kaoru Ishikawa, etc.), these broadly based philosophies do not include specific requirements. Instead they advocate change in the organization's philosophy on quality, management commitment, and organizational culture.

These organizations work to create a structured system for creating organization-wide participation in planning and implementing a continuous improvement process to meet and exceed customer needs. The basic principles include:

- Focusing on your customers and their needs
- Using data and data analysis to make decisions that continuously improve the processes that produce quality products and services
- Involving everyone, both as individuals and team members, in the improvement efforts
- Using systems thinking and integrated planning

Environmental Management

The success of ISO 9000 worldwide as a practical way for manufacturers to demonstrate that they meet an internationally recognized quality system standard has established the feasibility of a similar coordination effort in environmental management.

Following the process used in developing the ISO 9000 series, a family of environmental management standards is under development by ISO TC 207 on Environmental Management, with strong input from the United States and Canada. The structure and content of the work being done parallels ISO 9000 in many ways. Activities will include harmonizing auditor training criteria, as well as course provider and registrar accreditation processes as part of a coordinated quality management system.

In the United States there is planned organizational overlap of working groups that manage the development and administration of the standards, so that there will be a minimum of duplication of effort. On the next page is a list of the ISO TC 207 projected standards being developed. As of this printing, the initial standards are in draft stage.

As with ISO 9000, proposed environmental quality management standards will not dictate the actual standards to be met, such as for air and water quality, but will coordinate procedures for verifying that systems exist for controlling national environmental standards.

See the next page for a listing of the standards and their assigned numbers.

Environmental Management Standards Under Development or Projected

ISO 14000	Guidelines on principles, systems and supporting techniques
ISO 14001	Specification with guidance for use
ISO 14010-12	Auditing procedures
ISO 14020-24	Environmental labeling
ISO 14031	Environmental performance evaluation
ISO 14041-44	Life cycle assessment
ISO 14050	Terms and definitions
ISO 14060	Guide for environmental aspects in product standards

ISO TC 207 on Environmental Management Organizational Structure

WG 1	Environmental Aspects in Product Standards
SC 1	Environmental Management Systems
SC 2	Environmental Auditing and Related Environmental Investigations
SC 3	Environmental Labeling
SC 4	Environmental Performance Evaluation
SC 5	Life Cycle Assessment
SC 6	Terms and Definitions

SC = Subcommittee
WG = Working group

Chapter 5

Additional Resources

The ISO 9000 Standards Resources

International standards issued are available through the national standards body in each country.

United
States:
American National Standards Institute
11 W. 42nd Street
New York, NY 10036
Phone: (212) 642-4900 **Fax:** (212) 302-1286

Canada: **Canadian Standards Association**
178 Rexdale Boulevard
Rexdale (Toronto) Ontario
Canada M9W1R3
Phone: (416) 747-4040 **Fax:** (416) 747-2475

Many countries reissue and publish international standards as national standards under a separate designation. They are available from:

> **ASQC Quality Press**
> Customer Service Department
> 611 E. Wisconsin Avenue
> P. O. Box 3005
> Milwaukee, WI 53201-3005
> **Phone:** (800) 248-1946 **Fax:** (414) 272-1734

The headquarters for ISO is:

> **International Organization for Standardization**
> 1, rue de Varembé
> Case postale 56
> CH-1211 Genève 20
> Switzerland
> **Phone:** 41 22 749 01 11 **Fax:** 41 22 733 34 30

Supplements to QS-9000

Five customer reference manuals are referred to in QS-9000. The *Production Part Approval Process* manual is a requirement document. The other manuals are for guidance, to be made use of as appropriate.

Manual Title	QS-9000 Clause Reference
Production Part Approval Process	4.2.3
	4.4.9
	4.9.2
	4.9.6
Advanced Product Quality Planning and Control Plan	4.1.2
	4.2.3
Potential Failure Mode and Effects Analysis	4.2.3
Measurement System Analysis	4.11.4
Fundamental SPC	4.20.2

Note: *QS-9000 includes all text copy of clauses 4.1 through 4.20 of ISO 9001 verbatim.*

Copies of QS-9000 and reference manuals are available from:

Automotive Industry Action Group
26200 Lahser Road, Suite 200
Southfield, MI 48034
Phone: (810) 358-3003 **Fax:** (810) 358-3253

History of ISO 9000

The International Organization for Standardization (ISO) was formed in 1946 in Geneva, Switzerland. The ISO's intention was to promote the development of international standards and related activities so as to foster the increased trade of products and services between countries.

The ISO, made up of Technical Committees (TC), formed TC 176 specifically to address standardization issues relating to quality management and quality assurance. A subcommittee was established to determine common terminology, which was published in 1986 as ISO 8402. Another subcommittee was established to develop quality systems standards, the result being the ISO 9000 series published in 1987. Still another subcommittee was established to develop supplementary technical standards that were issued as additional standards in the ISO 9000, ISO 9004, and ISO 10000 series.

The ISO 9000 standards have been mandated by many governments and organizations around the world. Countries continue to have input into the ongoing development and improvement of the standards. According to ISO procedures, all ISO 9000 standards are reviewed and revised or reaffirmed once every five years.

TC 176 now has issued or is in the process of developing additional quality management and quality assurance standards, parts, and guidelines in the ISO 9000 and ISO 10000 series. These are listed on the following page. Use the key below to help you identify the status of documents.

> **DIS** = Draft international standard
> **CD** = Committee draft
> **WD** = Working draft

Quality Management and Quality Assurance Standards

Issued or being developed by ISO TC 176

Definitions of Key Terms and Acronyms

Accreditation is the formal recognition that a registration organization is competent to carry out the process of registration to the ISO 9000 standards/QS-9000 Requirements.

ANSI is the American National Standards Institute

ASQC is the American Society for Quality Control

Certificate is a written statement issued by a authorized body stating that an organization has complied with a set of standards or requirements.

Compliance is the affirmative indication or judgment that the supplier of a product or service has met the requirements of the relevant specifications, contract, or regulation.

Conformance: See compliance

Control chart is a graphical method for evaluating whether a process is or is not in a "state of statistical control."

CQI is Continuous Quality Improvement

CSA is the Canadian Standards Association

Design review is a formal, documented, comprehensive, and systematic examination of a design to evaluate the design requirements and the capability of the design to meet these requirements, and to identify problems and propose solutions.

Documentation is the systematic, orderly, and understandable descriptions and records of those policies and procedures affecting product and service quality.

EU is the European Union

EOQ is the European Organization for Quality

Inspection is the activities, such as measuring, examining, testing, gauging one or more characteristics of a product or service, and comparing these with specified requirements to determine conformity.

ISO is the International Organization for Standardization

Management review is the continual review of the quality system by management to make sure the quality system remains suitable and effective.

MBNQA is the Malcolm Baldrige National Quality Award

P_{pk} is the performance index, typically defined as the minimum

$$of \quad \frac{USL - \overline{\overline{X}}}{3\,\hat{\sigma}_s} \quad or \quad \frac{\overline{\overline{X}} - LSL}{3\,\hat{\sigma}_s}$$

Procedures are the documented practice(s) defining the who, what, and when of quality activities. Procedures are typically used at the departmental level, and may involve more than one department.

Process capability is the total range of inherent variation in a stable process.

Process control is the identification of and action on all factors affecting process variability, including materials accepted into the process, proper maintenance of equipment, use of statistical process control methods, and degree of adherence to work instructions.

Quality is the totality of features and characteristics of a product or service that bear on its ability to satisfy stated or implied needs of the customer(s).

Quality audit is the periodic review of the quality system by trained auditors, to ensure that quality activities meet requirements, and that the system is effective.

Quality assurance is all the planned and systematic activities implemented within a quality system that provide confidence that requirements for quality are being fulfilled.

Quality control is the operational techniques and activities used to fulfill requirements of quality.

Quality management is that aspect of the overall management function that determines and implements the quality policy.

Quality manual is the document stating the quality policy and describing the quality system of the organization. It should state the company's total commitment to quality.

Quality plan is a document setting out the specific quality practices, resources, and activities relevant to a particular product, process, service, contract, or project.

Quality policy is the overall intentions and direction of an organization in regards to quality as formally expressed by top management.

Quality system is the organizational structure, procedures, processes, and resources needed to implement quality management.

Registrar is the company that conducts quality system assessment to a recognized quality systems standard or set of requirements.

Registrar Accreditation Board is an affiliate of the ASQC that recognizes the competence and reliability of registrars of quality systems, and works to achieve international recognition of registrations issued by accredited registrars.

Registration is the procedure by which an organization indicates that it fulfills the requirements for a quality management system and then is included or registered in an appropriate public list.

Responsibility and Authority is the responsibility to prevent occurrence of product nonconformity; to identify and record any product quality problems; recommend solutions; verify their implementation; and control further

---

©1996 GOAL/QPC

processing; delivery or installation of nonconforming products until the problem has been corrected. The same individuals having responsibility should have the authority to carry out the responsibilities.

Specification is the document that prescribes the requirements that the product or service has to meet.

Statistical process control is the application of statistical techniques to the control of processes.

Statistical quality control is the application of statistical techniques to the control of quality.

Subcontractor is an organization that provides a product or service to the supplier.

Supplier is an organization that provides a product or service to the customer.

Surveillance is the continuing monitoring and verification of the status of procedures, methods, conditions, products, processes, and services, and analysis of records in relation to stated references to ensure that requirements for quality are being met.

Testing is a means of determining the capability of an item to meet specified requirements by subjecting the item to a set of physical, chemical, environmental, or operating actions and conditions.

Traceability is the ability to trace the history, application, or location of an item or activity and like items or activities by means of recorded identification.

TQM is Total Quality Management

References

- *Coach's Guide to The Memory Jogger™ II*, Michael Brassard, Diane Ritter, and others, GOAL/QPC, Methuen, MA, 1995.

- *Coach's Guide* Package. Includes the *Coach's Guide*, 5 copies of *The Memory Jogger™ II* and *The Learner's Reference Guide*, and 187 overhead transparencies.

- *Demystifying ISO 9000: Information Mapping's Guide to the ISO 9000 Standards*, Information Mapping, Waltham, MA, 1994.

- *Guide to Quality Control*, Kaoru Ishikawa, Asian Productivity Organization, Tokyo, 1982.

- *ISO 9000: Preparing for Registration*, James L. Lamprecht, Marcel Dekker, NY, 1992.

- *Process Quality Control: Troubleshooting and Interpretation of Data*, Ellis R. Ott and Edward G. Schilling, McGraw-Hill, NY, 1990.

- *The ISO 9000 Handbook*, Robert W. Peach, editor, Irwin Professional Publishing, Homewood, IL, 1994.

- *The Memory Jogger™ II*, Michael Brassard and Diane Ritter, GOAL/QPC, Methuen, MA, 1994.

- *The Memory Jogger™ Software* (Seven Quality Control Tools), GOAL/QPC, Methuen, MA, 1993.

- *The Memory Jogger Plus+® Software* (Seven Management & Planning Tools), GOAL/QPC, Methuen, MA, 1995.

- *The Team Memory Jogger™*, GOAL/QPC (Methuen, MA) and Joiner Associates (Madison, WI), 1995.

- *Using ISO 9000 to Improve Business Processes*, AT&T, 1994.

For a listing of more specialized reference books, see Chapter 3, page 136.

Notes

Customization of Your GOAL/QPC Books

Customize GOAL/QPC products with your company's name and logo, mission or vision statement, and almost anything else.

Benefits of customization
- Allows you more flexibility in determining content
- Gives your leaders an opportunity to personalize every copy
- Helps to promote your company's quality improvement efforts
- Communicates your organization's commitment to quality
- Helps lower the costs of in-house development of training materials
- Helps employees understand how they can help achieve company goals
- Gives your team a common vision

A few details
- Please allow a minimum of *4–6 weeks* for delivery of customized products.
- Customization is most cost effective for quantities of *200 or more.*
- Ask us about customizing GOAL/QPC products in other languages.
- We're flexible on what and how much can be customized; almost anything is possible. Just call us to find out!

The Memory Jogger™ II

This pocket guide—expanded and improved from the original *Memory Jogger*—is designed to help you improve the procedures, systems, quality, cost, and yields related to your job. *The Memory Jogger™ II* combines the basic Quality Tools and the Seven Management and Planning Tools in an easy-to-use format. It includes continuous improvement tools such as Cause and Effect, Histogram, Run Chart, Pareto Chart, and many more!

*Code: 1030E   Price: **$6.95***

The Team Memory Jogger™

Easy to read and written from the team member's point of view, *The Team Memory Jogger™* goes far beyond basic theories to provide you with practical nuts-and-bolts action steps on preparing to be an effective team member, how to get a good start, get work done in teams, and when and how to end a project. *The Team Memory Jogger™* also teaches you how to deal with problems that can arise within a team. It's perfect for all employees at all levels.

*Code: 1050E   Price: **$7.95***

Quantity discounts are available. Please call for details!

Ordering Information
Three Ways to Order

☎

Call Toll Free
1-800-643-4316
or 508-685-6370
8:30 AM – 5 PM EST

Fax
508-685-6151
Any day, any time

✉

Mail
GOAL/QPC
13 Branch Street
Methuen, MA 01844-1953

Price per copy		Shipping charges
1–9	$6.95	Continental U.S. 4% of order
10–49	$5.95	and handling charge of $4.00
50–99	$5.50	Alaska, Hawaii
100–499	$4.95	Canada
500–1999	$4.75	Puerto Rico
2000–2499	$4.50	Other countries

For quantities of 2500 or more, call for a quote.

Shipping charges (right column):
Continental U.S. 4% of order and handling charge of $4.00
Alaska, Hawaii
Canada
Puerto Rico   } Please call us
Other countries

Sales tax

Canada	7% of order
Georgia	Applicable tax
Massachusetts	5% of order
Pennsylvania	6% of order

Payment methods

We accept payment by check, money order, or credit card. Purchase orders are also accepted. **If you pay by purchase order:** 1) provide the name and address of the person to be billed, or 2) send a copy of the P.O. when order is payable by an agency of the federal government.

Order Form for The Memory Jogger™ 9000

1. Shipping Address (We cannot ship to a P.O. Box)

Name _____

Title _____

Company _____

Address _____

City _____

State _____ Zip _____ Country _____

Phone _____ Fax _____

E-Mail _____

2. Quantity & Price

Code	Quantity	Unit Price	Total Price
1060E			
		Tax MA,GA,PA & Canada only	
		Shipping Charge 4% of order (continental U.S. only)	
		Handling Fee	$4.00
		Total	

3. Payment Method

❒ Check enclosed (payable to GOAL/QPC) $ _____

❒ VISA ❒ MasterCard ❒ Amex ❒ Diners Club ❒ Discover

Card # _____ Exp. date _____

Signature _____

❒ Purchase order # _____

Bill to _____

Address _____

City _____

State _____ Zip _____ Country _____

4. Request for Other Materials

❒ Information on products, courses & training

We'd Like to Know What You Think of The Memory Jogger™ 9000 . . .

Your opinions about this product are important to u
Please return your completed survey by mail or fax
GOAL/QPC, attention Memory Jogger 9000. Thank yo

1. **How did you hear about this new book?**

- ❏ GOAL/QPC Product Catalog
- ❏ At a conference/expo
- ❏ Coworker
- ❏ Magazine advertisement
- ❏ Purchased original *Memory Jogger*™
- ❏ Other _____

2. **What do you like most about this book?**

3. **How will you use this book? Check all that apply.**

- ❏ Training class text
- ❏ Post-training reference
- ❏ Personal reference
- ❏ Coaching/mentoring
- ❏ Other _____

4. **How can we make this a better product for you?**

- ❏ Please add my name to your mailing list.
- ❏ I prefer not to be added to your mailing list.

Name _____

Title _____

Company _____

Address _____

City _____

State _____ Zip _____ Country _____

Phone _____ Fax _____

E-Mail _____